TRUE STORIES
OF
THE SAS

ROBIN HUNTER

This revised and updated edition first published
in Great Britain in 1995 by
Virgin Books
an imprint of Virgin Publishing Ltd
Thames Wharf Studios
Rainville Road, London W6 9HT

First published in Great Britain in 1985

Reprinted 1997, 1998

A catalogue record for this book is available from the
British Library

ISBN 0 86369 912 X

Typeset by TW Typesetting, Plymouth, Devon

Printed and bound by
Caledonian International Book Manufacturing Ltd, Glasgow

CONTENTS

ACKNOWLEDGEMENTS

The author gratefully acknowledges the assistance of the Public Record Office; the National Army Museum; the Imperial War Museum; the Royal Marines Museum, Portsmouth; the Parachute Regiment Museum, Aldershot; the London Library; the Newspaper Library, Colindale; and Terry Brown, late of 42 Commando.

There's a legion that never was listed,
That carries no colours or crest,
But split in a thousand detachments,
Is paving a way for the rest.

CHRONOLOGY

July 1941:
: The SAS, then designated 'L' Detachment, raised in Egypt by Lt David Stirling. Total strength six officers, 60 NCOs and men.

Nov. 1941–Jan. 1943:
: SAS patrols raid German and Italian airfields and installations in the Western Desert, destroying over 250 aircraft on the ground. Stirling, now Lt-Col, captured Jan. 1943. SAS direction and control now extends to 1st and 2nd SAS Regt: the Special Raiding Squadron (SRS) and the Special Boat Section (SBS), plus Allied Special Force Units.

1943/4/5:
: SAS and SRS/SBS raids in Italy and the Greek Islands.

1944–5:
: SAS parachute into France before D-Day. SAS order of battle for D-Day:

HQ SAS Brigade

```
                    HQ SAS Brigade
        ┌──────────────┴──────────────┐
    1st SAS Regt                   2nd SAS Regt
        │                              │
3rd (French) SAS Regt      │   4th (French) SAS Regt
                    1st (Belgian) SAS Squadron
```

Oct. 1945:	British SAS Regiments disbanded.
1949:	21 SAS Regt (TA) (Artists), a territorial unit, raised and based in London.
1950:	Maj J. M. Calvert raises the Malaya Scouts to fight Chinese Communist terrorists in Malaya.
1951:	The Malaya Scouts and M Squadron 21 SAS combine to form 22 SAS.
1952–7:	22 SAS in Malaya.
1958–76:	22 SAS serve in the Gulf, in Oman, Dhufar, Aden.
1963–5:	22 SAS serve in Borneo during 'confrontation' with Indonesia.
1970–82:	SAS deployed in counter-terrorist role in Northern Ireland, Britain and elsewhere.
1982:	The SAS in the Falklands War.
1982–94:	The SAS serve in Ulster and standby. The CRW serve at Hereford.
1991:	The SAS in 'Desert Storm'.

INTRODUCTION
WHAT IS THE SAS?

Until one day in May 1980 it is fair to say that few people outside the enclosed world of the British army had even heard of the SAS Regiment. Then, thanks to the presence of television cameras and the assembled mass media, the regiment sprang to the attention of the world. For the past week, the staff of the Iranian Embassy had been held hostage by a group of Iranian dissidents. Whether they were terrorists or patriots, the situation could not continue, and when one of the hostages was killed, the regiment moved in.

Black-hooded figures came abseiling dramatically down the walls of the Iranian Embassy. Swinging on ropes, they crashed through the windows. Then came explosions, gushes of flame, short bursts of gunfire and a siege that had electrified and infuriated television audiences for a week or more came to a sudden and bloody close. The SAS Regiment, to which these mysterious soldiers belonged, became the talk of the town, if not the world; the very stuff of adventure and romance.

The Special Air Service Regiment had then been in existence for nearly 40 years and served with distinction in every corner of the world. Now everyone wanted to know their story.

Writing the story of this unique regiment presents a problem, even when the writer concentrates on published and available facts. The Special Air Service Regiment does not like publicity, either for its men or its activities.

Such reticence is largely dictated by its current role as a counter-terrorist and surveillance unit, but while such secrecy is understandable, it does give rise to speculation which can be unfounded and is often unfair.

During the research for this book I was assured by one journalist 'as a fact', that most SAS troopers were 'psychopaths, trained to kill anyone'. Another, of a more left-wing persuasion, described the SAS as 'Maggie's Muscle ... and we'll disband them when the next Socialist government comes to power.' This seems unlikely. In the present world most governments find it necessary to maintain a striking force against the ungodly; in many countries, such a force is drawn from the police, but Britain has chosen the military path and the counter-terrorist role in the UK is filled by the SAS. As a regiment, the SAS have powerful friends and many enemies, so one might do worse than set the record straight at the beginning and make it clear exactly what the SAS Regiment is, who joins it, what its role is and where it fits in the military world and contemporary society.

The 22 SAS Regiment is a unit of the British army. The men who join it are regular serving soldiers of the British army who apply for SAS selection and training (for more details see Chapter 12). If accepted they join the regiment for a few years, in the case of the officers or, if they wish, for the rest of their service in the case of NCOs and other ranks.

The SAS selection and training course, in the harsh damp terrain of the Black Mountains and the Brecon Beacons around Hereford, of which much has been written, has been designed to weed out unsuitable types and select the best possible recruits for service with the SAS. It also shows potential recruits exactly what they are up against should they be selected for service. The SAS themselves are keen to point out that rejection is no reflection on a man's ability as a soldier. The SAS role requires certain personal qualities which are demanded by the tasks they undertake. SAS troopers usually work in small close-knit groups, and not infrequently alone. A man might serve

2

with distinction in the artillery, the tanks or the line infantry, and yet find the SAS role not at all to his taste.

It is also fair to point out that, certainly in the early days, many SAS soldiers were misfits in their original regiments. One of their most distinguished officers, Blair 'Paddy' Mayne, was under close arrest for striking his superior officer when recruited to serve in the original SAS.

Gerald Bryan, an officer of No. 11 Commando remembers Paddy Mayne well:

Blair Mayne was an Ulsterman, a natural soldier, a born fighting man. He never really settled down in the peace. When sober a nicer, a gentler, or more mild mannered man you could not wish to meet but when drunk or in battle he was frightening.

I am not saying he was a drunk, but he could drink a bottle of whisky in the evening before he got a glow on. He also had great physical strength, stood six feet four inches tall and had been both a boxer and a rugby international.

I remember one night when he had been on the bottle he literally picked me up off the floor by the lapels of my tunic and punched me with the other hand, sending me flying across the room. Next day he could not remember a thing about it. He saw my face and my black eye and said, 'Tell me who did that to you, Gerald.' I told him I had walked into a door. He was a very brave man and I liked him very much.

After joining the SAS, Paddy Mayne went on to win four DSOs and become the most decorated British soldier in the Second World War. As far as the SAS are concerned it is 'horses for courses', and they aim to find, train and command disciplined soldiers, suited to a testing and highly specialised role.

The SAS Regiment has now survived for over 50 years of peace and war, overcoming disbandment, amalgamations and a steady erosion of service manpower that has reduced the size of the British army and eliminated many famous regiments, because it has always been willing to adapt to circumstances and can always find a fresh and useful role in a changing but never peaceful world.

This basic role has changed considerably since the regiment was originally formed in 1941, but the character remains much the same. SAS soldiers are trained as a small-scale fighting force suited to raiding, reconnaissance, deep penetration behind hostile lines, intelligence gathering and close-quarter combat. Constant adaptability has been the main reason for the regiment's revival and survival; whatever the nature of the threat facing the country at home or abroad, the SAS had adjusted to counter it. In the Western Desert they raided enemy airfields and logistical centres, destroying the enemy's fixed bases and supply routes. In the post-war campaigns of Malaya, Borneo, Oman, Northern Ireland or the Arabian Gulf the SAS found a role in pursuing the terrorists – or 'guerrillas' or 'freedom fighters' – to their strongholds. As the Empire ended and terrorism raised its ugly head in the West, the SAS adapted their role yet again. When all else fails, when other methods of persuasion have been exhausted, they and their colleagues in the counter-terrorist special force units of other democratic nations become *Ultimo ratio regis* – the 'King's Last Argument' – a noted, implacable force.

At the end of the day, even democratic nations have to be prepared to use force against those who choose to ignore the rules of civilised society or go outside the law to make their case. Given the limitations of the democratic process, and that even the terrorist, the gunman and the subversive must be given a fair crack of the whip and justice under the law – rights that they usually deny to others – this force, when used, must be used sparingly, accurately, and with the minimum effect on innocent bystanders. Although this aim has not always been achieved, it is in this delicate application of force that the SAS has proved most useful over the last two decades.

As the soldiers might put it, the SAS don't 'muck about'. Once deployed, their role is to strike the enemy hard, and since taking prisoners must be a secondary consideration in such circumstances, when the SAS are called in to resolve a situation the end is often swift, violent and bloody. On the other hand, the SAS have learned to work with local people, practise 'hearts and minds' techniques as a matter of course, learn native languages, eat local food and offer medical advice to the people among whom they soldier.

Their aim is to avoid the use of force until and unless it is absolutely necessary. The SAS were among the first to realise the importance of using the 'hearts and minds' of the local population, and thereby their support, during the Malayan Emergency of the 1950s and 1960s, and they have applied the techniques they learned there ever since.

When General Templar, then commanding British forces in the Malayan Emergency declared that 'the solution to countering the Communist threat lies not in putting more troops into the jungle, but putting democracy into the hearts and minds of the local people', the SAS were among the first regiments to apply that principle.

Wherever they are deployed, they work with the local people, helping with schools, civic works and medical aid and conforming to the local customs and habits. Their selection of the right techniques for any given situation is another well honed SAS skill; hand-to-hand combat is not the principal skill of an SAS soldier.

To carry out their tasks with success demands a high level of skill and nerve – achieved by constant specialised training. Yet despite their current mystique, and the acclaim of the media, the SAS trooper is not a superman. Any regiment recruited exclusively from 'heroes' would be a very small force indeed. It is the basic qualities of character, self-discipline and a high state of fitness backed by constant training and regular experience of high-risk situations which give the SAS soldier his fighting edge, rather than any willingness to expose life and limb carelessly to hazard.

In the last few years the basic purpose of this unique and very British regiment has become obscured by extravagant tales in the media. Some of these tales are highly suspect, and some of the characters who claim to have served in the SAS have never been within a mile of Hereford. This account aims to avoid hyperbole and tell the story of the SAS as it really is; sensible, useful, soldierly. It will also give a clear answer to the question: 'What is the SAS?' It charts the SAS through a wide variety of roles, each an adaptation of a basic technique, each drawing strength and purpose from the guiding ideals of the regiment – discipline, training, fitness, expertise. These qualities may not be glamorous, but they achieve results.

The book is not a regimental history but a series of stories, each set into the context of a larger, longer campaign, which will illustrate the changing roles of a unique British regiment from the dark days of 1941 to the ever-doubtful days of the mid-1980s. The true story of a regiment is told in deeds rather than words, and the SAS would surely prefer it that way.

PROLOGUE

BEGINNINGS IN THE DESERT
1940–1

The Western Desert, and the mountains of Tunisia, where the North African campaign of 1940–3 was fought out, is a vast, bleak, waterless place, almost the size of India. Along the coastal strip, which runs for some 1500 miles from Tunis to Cairo, the land is irrigated and cultivated and contains a number of towns, each of which became a landmark on the maps of the Desert War: Tobruk, Mersa Matruh, Agheila, Benghazi, Sirte, Tripoli. Behind that coastal strip lies the desert and to the north lies the Mediterranean; both hemming in the fertile, populated coast, both a path for invading armies or raiding forces.

In 1940–1 the British forces enjoyed considerable success against the mainly Italian enemy, driving them to and fro across the desert in a series of advances and retreats that became known among the troops as the 'Benghazi Handicap'. Then, in the spring of 1941, the Germans, fearing defeat for their Italian allies, despatched to the desert a formidable expeditionary force, the doughty 'Afrika Korps', under a general who was to become famous among both the Axis and Allied armies: Field Marshal Erwin Rommel.

In ten days of April and May 1941 Rommel drove the British back in full retreat up to the frontiers of Egypt. The Allied position became desperate, for if Egypt fell so would the Suez Canal, the oil countries of the Middle East, the beleaguered island of Malta – Britain's last outpost in the central Mediterranean. Even India would be vulnerable if Egypt could not be held. To hold Egypt was vital, but Rommel was seemingly invincible.

There was, however, one small shred of hope. The Desert War was very much a war of logistics, of supply. In war, the supply factor can be as crucial as the results of the actual fighting – and in the Western Desert, campaign after campaign petered out as each army outran its supply line. All the stores and equipment, German as well as British, had to be transported first by sea or air to North Africa, and then to and fro along and across the coastal plain. These long supply lines were very vulnerable to disruption by raiding forces and before long the British began to produce small-scale irregular units, often commanded by rather eccentric soldiers, usually with less than military names: Popski's Private Army and the Long Range Desert Group were just two of the most famous and effective, but there were also 'Jock Columns' provided by the regular army, roving patrols from units like the 11th Hussars, and Commando raids by a brigade of British troops known as Layforce. Their routes towards the vulnerable store depots and supply lines were the wide deserts which lay south of the coast or the Mediterranean sea. Curiously enough, the Germans never developed similar formations and this sea of sand remained the preserve of British raiding forces throughout the years of the Desert War.

There was, however, a problem: mobility. Raiding forces require mobility both to strike and to get away again. This in part limits their numbers, but the problem was acute in the Western Desert in 1941 because the British army was dangerously short of transport and all manner of other resources. To get to their targets, the special forces could choose between the air, the sea or the land, but the sea route was exposed to German air power, and ships caught off the North African coast in daylight did not stay afloat for long. A shortage of transport aircraft and parachutes limited the air option, and that left the desert below the coastal plain.

The coastal plain was not wide, perhaps 50 miles at the

most, and the vast sand seas of North Africa to the south, where armies could not manoeuvre, was a waterless place of dust, heat and flies. In this wilderness, however, small, specialist, raiding and reconnaissance units did manage to move and in this unguarded expanse of frontier a young British second-lieutenant saw an opportunity.

1

THE SAS IN THE DESERT WAR

When the Second World War broke out in 1939, David Stirling, the founder of the SAS, was climbing in the Rocky Mountains, training for an attempt on the summit of Everest. Stirling was a Scot, the scion of an aristocratic family, educated conventionally at Ampleforth and Cambridge. He returned home in 1939 and enlisted in the Scots Guards, where he remained until the end of 1940 when he joined No. 8 Commando, which then sailed for Egypt as part of a Commando Brigade commanded by Colonel Robert Laycock and known therefore as Layforce.

Commando forces were a new idea at the time and were being raised in some quantity as a means of learning and improving the techniques of amphibious warfare with which to raid the long coastlines of occupied Europe and to spearhead the eventual Allied invasion of the Continent.

Layforce was sent to the Mediterranean to carry the war to the Italians and Germans along the southern front, but a shortage of shipping and the complete failure of the higher command in the Middle East to realise their potential brought all the good intentions of Brigadier Laycock to nothing. As a result, Layforce was never employed in the Desert War, largely because it could not be transported into action. There were no ships available and no suitable target small enough to be captured or large enough to warrant the employment of a full brigade. The regiments in the Western Desert were short of men, and before long greedy eyes were cast upon Laycock's brigade of trained soldiers. Gradually Layforce began to disintegrate as men either returned to their parent units or were sent to reinforce infantry battalions in the line. Those who had joined the commandos in the hope of swift action were bitterly disappointed.

Meanwhile, an officer of 8 Commando, Jock Lewes, had laid his hands on some parachutes and invited Stirling and some others to try them out. A highly unsuitable aircraft was acquired from the Royal Air Force and their jumping trials near Mersa Matruh were hazardous in the extreme. The aircraft was not equipped for parachuting and the men secured their 'static lines', which pull the parachute canopy from the pack, by simply lashing the lines to seats near the aircraft door. The result was inevitable: Stirling's parachute caught and ripped on exit. He descended far too rapidly and hit the desert with considerable force, severely injuring his back and legs. For some days it was thought he would be permanently paralysed, but after a week or two in bed he began to recover.

Stirling's stay in hospital gave him time to think, to put some ideas on paper, and consider the problems of getting at the enemy. The desert, as he saw it, was like the open sea, unguarded and unguardable. If men could be dropped into the desert by parachute, surely they could infiltrate the enemy supply lines, destroying dumps, airfields and tank depots. The desert was indeed like a sea, on which small units could move at will, undetected, striking hard and then fading away into the waste of sand. He scribbled furiously, his bed covered with maps and notebooks, and by the time he limped out of hospital he had a plan ready to present to the commanding generals. The generals unfortunately, were not interested. They had a full-scale war to fight and other things to do with their time than listen to a guards officer who should have been with his parent battalion and not messing about with parachutes and hare-brained schemes for special forces.

Stirling finally brought his proposals to the attention of the authorities by shinning over a barbed-wire fence, evading sentries at GHQ and accosting General Ritchie, the deputy chief of staff, in his office. Somewhat to Stirling's surprise, especially after all the previous resistance, his idea of a small-scale raiding force was now accepted with alacrity. He was given permission to assemble six officers and 60 men, to be impressively entitled 'L Detachment, The SAS Brigade'. The SAS stood for Special Air Service, which did not exist, but Intelligence officers on the general staff wished Rommel to believe that strong British parachute forces had arrived in the Middle East. Whatever happened to his raiding forces in action, Stirling's parachute activity, when training in the Delta, would certainly be spotted by Axis spies and help to aid this deception.

Stirling recruited his force inside a week, mostly from Layforce and the Brigade of Guards. His officers included Jock Lewes and a man who was soon to rank among the great fighting soldiers of the war, the Ulsterman, Paddy Mayne. The infant SAS set up camp at Kabrit, on the edge of the Suez Canal, and began to train hard and in earnest.

From the start Stirling insisted on a high standard of discipline and turn-out, with the rider that once operations started these could be relaxed. Training consisted of long, 30 mile marches into the desert on one bottle of water per man per day, plenty of PT to gain that essential fitness, and weapon training which included familiarisation with all kinds of weapons, German and Italian as well as British. Much of this training took place at night since the SAS raiders would most often be operating under cover of darkness. As getting to the objective was the first task, everyone had to be parachute trained.

Stirling had the parachutes, but no RAF instructors were available, so the SAS developed their own parachute training techniques, jumping from ever-higher platforms or from the backs of lorries moving at 30 miles an hour. These methods did not always prove wise. Broken ankles, bruised shoulders or wrenched backs soon became commonplace, and everyone was relieved when they finally moved on to the actual jumping – from Bristol Bombays, an obsolescent bomber-type aircraft then going out of service.

The parachutes used by military paratroops are not of the free-fall variety. To prevent the force being scattered widely on the ground, paratroops usually drop from a low altitude and their chutes are opened – or 'deployed' – by a static line from the chute which is attached to a wire inside the aircraft. Stirling led the first two jumps, of twelve men each time, and then stayed on the ground to watch the aircraft approach for the next drop.

The first two men jumped but their parachutes failed to open, and the third was stopped just in time by the horrified RAF despatcher. The aircraft circled away and landed its shocked cargo of troops for a hurried inquest, in which it was discovered that a safety clip which should have stopped the static line-hook twisting loose from the wire had somehow been omitted. New clips were fitted and next day the aircraft took off again, Stirling sitting by the door to lead the jump. When the red and green lights came on Stirling led his men out of the door. This time, all the parachutes opened safely, and with their training thus dramatically completed, the SAS were ready for action.

With their training completed, the SAS were now ready for their first raid, but Stirling decided that a dress rehearsal would be advisable. Stirling therefore sharpened his men for their first operation with a training raid on the large RAF base at Heliopolis outside Cairo. Although the airfield guards had been warned of their coming, daily aircraft reconnaissance over the desert had failed to detect the approach of the raiders and the perimeter guards and patrols could not keep them out. The SAS marched 90 miles across the desert in three nights, hiding under sacks during the day, tormented by flies and heat and thirst. On the third night they penetrated the airfield defences and placed labels representing bombs on 45 aircraft before fading away quietly into the darkness. The RAF was not amused, and airfield security was promptly reinforced. This Stirling regarded as irrelevant; given the advantage of surprise, the trained raider will always get through.

The first real attack was scheduled for the night of 17 November 1941, when five SAS groups would parachute into the desert near Gazala and attack the five forward German airfields. 'With luck,' Stirling told his troops, to wild applause, 'we'll wipe out the entire German fighter force.' But their luck, alas, was out.

Parachuting demands good weather and light winds, but on the morning of 16 November 1941 the weather already looked ominous. The wind was already strong and rain was forecast, the wind soon rising to a full gale. In spite of this, Stirling decided to launch his force, partly because the higher authorities in Cairo expected it, and partly because many of his men had joined the SAS in disgust at the cancellation of other operations. To call off this one might be very bad for morale, so in spite of the weather he ordered it to proceed.

As was then the custom, the men were to jump unarmed, their weapons and explosives packed into containers which would be dropped separately, and not, as now, attached to the men by rope. At dusk, men and containers were loaded into five Bombays and the aircraft set off into the sunset, first heading out to sea, then turning inland to cross the coast well behind the German lines. The aircraft were bucketing wildly in the storm, and the ground below was totally obscured by darkness and the whirling sandstorm.

The drop itself was a disaster. Stirling records jumping out and then waiting and waiting for the shock of landing as the wind sent his parachute soaring above the surface of the desert. When the landing shock finally came, it knocked him senseless. He recovered to stagger about in a maelstrom of wind and driven sand, unable to see, his shouts drowned by the ceaseless roar of the storm, his raiding force scattered across the desert in the howling night.

It took hours for the group to assemble. One trooper

and eight of the ten weapons containers were missing and never found. Virtually unarmed, their supplies and explosives missing, there was nothing to do but call off the attack and attempt to walk out to the British lines, avoiding captivity if possible, heading for a rendezvous 40 miles deeper in the desert where a motor patrol of the Long Range Desert Group (LRDG) was awaiting them.

It took several days for the SAS, split into small parties, to reach the LRDG rendezvous and some never made it. When Stirling arrived and counted his troops, he had four officers and 18 men left out of the force of seven officers and 45 men who had jumped into the storm three nights before. One abortive operation had virtually wiped out the SAS in their first action. Any other man might have given up the whole idea.

2

SAS AND LRDG

Fortunately for Stirling, the Eighth Army generals had more to think about at that time than the misfortunes of a few parachute troops. The main counter-offensive against Rommel was not going well against tough German resistance, and when Rommel's inevitable counter-attack came in, the Eighth Army supply lines again became extended. Rommel therefore threw the British back and actually penetrated the frontiers of Egypt. While all this was going on, Stirling withdrew with the remains of his band to the remote oasis at Jalo, to recruit more men and rethink his tactics.

Clearly, parachuting was too hit-or-miss for sustained raiding, but one possible source of transportation might lie with his new-found friends, the LRDG. The Long Range Desert Group had been operating in the Western Desert for most of the war, essentially as a reconnaissance unit behind the Axis lines, reporting back to GHQ on enemy strengths, movements and position, though they could, and did, attack the enemy when the opportunity presented itself. Stirling suggested that they might add transporting his SAS raiders to their list of tasks and the LRDG took to the idea at once. 'Of course we'll help,' they told him. 'You tell us where you want to go and we'll take you there, and bring you back.' Stirling gathered his officers together and began to brood over his maps.

In the next few months this happy conjunction of SAS and LRDG brought death and destruction to the enemy.

LRDG patrols carried the SAS far behind the enemy lines, letting them off to raid airfields and supply depots, and providing transport for wild raids along the coastal road, where the SAS were able to attack enemy transport and troop movements almost at will, shooting up any camp or transport park that loomed up in the night. Before long SAS patrols were in action every night, the crash of their bombs and the glow of the fires they started becoming familiar features of night-time in the desert. Many SAS soldiers found raiding very much to their taste and became 'one-man waves of destruction' once loose behind the enemy lines.

On one occasion, Paddy Mayne attacked the fighter airfield at Sirte, destroyed 24 aircraft and took the time before leaving to gatecrash a party in the German officers' mess and spray the revellers with bullets from his tommygun. He then paused to destroy one final aircraft on the way out and, having run out of bullets and explosives, crippled the aircraft by tearing out its control panel with his bare hands. Jock Lewes raided a roadhouse and transport park, shooting the drivers and placing bombs on twelve petrol and tank transporters; Bill Fraser took a small patrol into the airfield at Agebadia and destroyed 37 aircraft – without the loss of a man. These raids proved highly effective. Every aircraft they destroyed, every litre of petrol they burned, had been brought at some cost across the Mediterranean, and it would take another painful voyage before these items could be replaced. The Germans and Italians, quite understandably, became seriously concerned.

After this first flurry of activity the pace steadied, but the attacks continued, gaining in strength and audacity as the SAS honed up their techniques. Mayne went to the airfield at Tamit and destroyed 27 aircraft, while Stirling took his own patrol – in LRDG transport – for an excursion down the main coast road, blowing up trucks, machine-gunning troop encampments, setting vehicles on fire and having a high old time. The SAS path was marked by a long swathe of destruction; but they had their own losses, some of them severe.

Enemy aircraft roamed the desert skies after each attack, seeking and sometimes finding the SAS and LRDG patrols which they then attacked relentlessly with machine-gun and cannon fire.

Jock Lewes attacked Nofilia, but during the withdrawal his patrol was spotted and attacked by fighters. Jock was killed and his patrol forced to disperse as more enemy aircraft arrived to bomb and strafe the survivors. Bill Fraser and his patrol had slightly better luck, but missed their LRDG rendezvous and had to walk home, trudging for eight days across 200 miles of hot, waterless, enemy-infested desert. They nearly died of thirst but, eventually, made the Eighth Army lines and rejoined the SAS at Kabrit.

The SAS were not under divisional command, or a private army. Stirling had realised right from the start that the continued existence and success of his creation depended on support from higher authority. Many of the raids described above were organised by Stirling and his officers without reference to higher authority, but they fitted in with his overall brief to cause destruction and consternation behind the enemy lines. The SAS were also strategic troops, reporting directly to Eighth Army headquarters, and, from time to time, the Eighth Army would have some particular task which they wished the SAS to perform as a matter of strategic necessity. One of these was to ease the pressure on the supply convoys from Britain which fought their way east up the Mediterranean under attack all the way from German and Italian aircraft. Anything that could be done to ease the passage of these vital convoys helped the Allied effort in the Western Desert.

After some months' successful raiding behind the German lines and a mounting score of enemy aircraft destroyed, the reputation of the SAS stood very high at Middle East headquarters. Stirling was promoted to Major and allowed to increase his forces, although he was not permitted to draw recruits from experienced front-line battalions, which restricted his plans considerably. Stirling insisted on a minimum of three months' training in SAS work for green troops fresh from the UK, which paid off in action but inevitably restricted the expansion of the regiment. However, the SAS exercised a magnetic attraction for all manner of men and Stirling soon had sufficient troops available to raid continually in the desert and expand his field of operations to enemy installations in Crete and the Greek Islands.

In May 1942, after six months in the field, Stirling was summoned to Middle East headquarters to discuss a Combined Operation being set up to aid the beleaguered garrison of Malta. Malta was the key to the war in the Middle East; it denied the enemy free passage for ships and men from Italy to North Africa. From Malta, British aircraft, submarines and destroyers crept out each night to sink ships and shoot down transport aircraft. If the Middle East war was to be won, Malta had to be held.

The Germans and Italians were well aware of this; they had been pounding Malta from the air for two long years. Every British convoy bringing supplies from Gibraltar endured a long calvary of air attack as they fought their way east under the pitiless blue of the Mediterranean sky. But without these convoys, costly though they were, Malta would surely fall. In May 1942 supplies were once again desperately low and, Stirling was informed, a fresh convoy was being assembled in Gibraltar and would sail for Malta in the middle of June. Could his men raid every German airfield they could reach and destroy as many enemy aircraft, especially bombers, as possible? Anything that reduced air attacks on the convoy would help the gallant garrison of the island fortress of Malta.

Stirling was back within a day with a complete plan. The SAS would raid eight separate bomber airfields in mid-June, seven on the African shore, one at Heraklion in Crete. Each raiding force would consist of five SAS men and the newly-formed French SAS, under Commander Berge, would have responsibility for the attacks on Derna, Barce and Crete. This would be the first operation for the French SAS, but another sign of Stirling's expanding command. There would eventually be French and Belgian SAS units, and in post-war years the SAS would draw their recruits from as far afield as New Zealand, Rhodesia and Fiji, a process that began in 1942 here in the Western Desert. It took a week to collect the supplies and brief the men, but on 6 June the SAS left Kabrit for their various destinations. All attacks were timed to take place on the nights of 14 and 15 June, when the convoy would be setting sail from Gibraltar.

Even now, after barely seven months' existence, the SAS had become the focus for irregular warfare in the Middle East. The French SAS patrol, heading for the Derna airfields, were accompanied by another curious force of irregulars, the SIG (Special Interrogation Group), a unit formed from German-speaking Palestinian Jews. The SIG carried deception to fine limits, wearing German uniforms, carrying German weapons and parading for German drill. They had also recruited two Afrika Korps German prisoners, who claimed to be fiercely anti-Nazi, as drill instructors, and this was to prove their downfall. One of these ex-prisoners left the patrol near Derna, ostensibly to recce the airfield – returning to assure them that all was clear. However, the patrol had been betrayed, and as they entered the field they ran into an ambush and were quickly surrounded.

Even so, the SAS and the SIG decided to fight, hurling grenades at their attackers, driving them back with bursts of tommy-gun fire. Lieutenant Jordan, a French SAS officer, had been captured but broke free and ran through the shooting and eventually made his way back to the Allied lines. Seven other Frenchmen escaped the ambush on the airfield and returned to their rendezvous in the desert, but this too had been betrayed by the SIG's Afrika Korps recruits. The SAS were surrounded again, this time by a company of Germany infantry, but again they decided to put up a fight. Only one of the French SAS returned to Kabrit after the Derna raid, and of that entire patrol all the rest were captured, wounded or killed. All the SIGs taken prisoner were shot by firing squad.

Meanwhile, Stirling and Mayne were attacking the three airfields around Benghazi, with considerable success. Bombs were placed on aircraft around the airfield, other bombs were used to destroy workshops and, as a parting touch, Stirling tossed a grenade into the guard-room, holding the door shut against the frantic occupants till it went off. As they left the scene the whole airfield exploded into flame. Mayne was up to similar tricks at the Berka satellite airfield which, having been raided before, was now heavily guarded.

Fortunately, to ease the problem of guarding the aircraft against SAS attacks, the Germans had grouped them together rather than keeping them well dispersed, and so the SAS were able to spread their bombs about most usefully, before they were detected and the firing started. They withdrew as the bombs went off, to be chased for miles across the desert by German mobile patrols in half-tracked trucks. The third Benghazi airfield was assailed by Lt Zirnheld, another French officer, who destroyed eleven bombers and then gave battle to the guards in the middle of the landing ground before disappearing into the night. The veteran SAS soldiers felt that this last touch was showing the right spirit.

This alone might seem a good score for any operation, but when the SAS troopers reassembled at their rendezvous, Stirling and Mayne felt that the night was still young and something else might yet be attempted. Taking a few of their cronies and borrowing a brand new truck from the LRDG on the strict understanding that they would return it without a scratch, they set out for the coast road. Within minutes they ran slap into a well-armed and thoroughly awake German roadblock.

They got through this by bluff and, once through, the troops in the back opened fire on the German sentries. Then the party set off on another of their wild rides along the coast road, machine-gunning roadhouses, blowing up petrol dumps, stores and tank-transporters before turning off into the desert, with German half-tracks now in hot pursuit. These they shook off, and were bumping happily home across the desert to their LRDG rendezvous when there came an urgent cry from the back. 'Get out! Quick! One of the bomb fuses is burning.' No one waited for the truck to stop and as the last man leapt clear, it exploded. 'What was left of it,' said one man, 'could have gone into a haversack.' Ever-forgiving, the LRDG sent a patrol to pick them up and they all returned safely to the oasis at Siwa.

The SAS raid on Crete was led by Commander Berge and Lord George Jellicoe, an officer who had transferred to the SAS from yet another irregular raiding unit, the Special Boat Section (SBS). This patrol went to Crete by submarine, landing on the coast east of Heraklion on 12 June. When they reached their observation point overlooking the airfield, they counted over 60 German bombers on the landing strip, and as soon as it grew dark, they set off down the mountain to attack. They cut a hole in the security fence and had put bombs on twenty aircraft before a German patrol discovered the cut fence, began to investigate and chased them away.

Two days later the Germans surrounded the SAS troopers in a cave high in the hills. Once again the French decided to fight it out and continued to fight until they ran out of ammunition. Only Jellicoe and a Greek guide were able to evade capture and, some days later, they rejoined the submarine waiting off the coast.

The total score of the eight SAS raids on the bomber stations came to 37 bombers definitely destroyed, plus a good deal of subsidiary damage to aircraft, spares and equipment. The Malta convoy sailed from Gibraltar in mid-June: out of seventeen ships which set out, only two survived to reach the harbour of Valletta, but that was enough to keep Malta supplied until another larger convoy fought its way through in July. The story of the Malta convoys is another epic of the Middle East campaign, and the terrible losses the crews sustained serve to indicate that heroism was not confined to the raiders of the SAS.

By now, in mid-1942, the SAS had been in existence for just over seven months. In that short space of time they had established a solid reputation, were growing in strength all the time, and were in a state of continual change.

Stirling became a Lieutenant-Colonel and Paddy Mayne a Major. The size of the SAS proper was now about 100 trained men, but Stirling was also given command of the Special Boat Section, what was left of 'Layforce', and a Greek Special Service unit known as the 'Sacred Squadron', so that the total force at his disposal approached 800 men. In addition, his brother Bill Stirling had been given permission to raise another SAS Regiment, the 2nd SAS, in England, and take it to the Middle East. Clearly, the SAS idea was catching on.

The commando and the parachute regiments were also expanding at this time, and the new Combined Operations headquarters was beginning to take an active interest in all special force units. Many of the irregular units that had sprung up in the last couple of years did not welcome the thought of overall control. Most of them had joined – or even formed – these special force units exactly to get away from the dead hand of higher authority, but they eventually made the discovery that even special force units have to be administered. Fighting and raiding may have been their prime purpose, but the effective execution of these enjoyable tasks could not be carried out without administrative and logistical back-up.

Men had to be recruited and trained; once recruited they had to be paid and clothed and sent on courses; vehicles, ammunition and other supplies had to be indented for; and there was a need to liaise with the air force, the navy or other units in the preparation and mounting of attacks. For the moment, the units were able to carry on much as before, but the time was coming when the growing number of special force units would have to be organised on a proper basis.

Stirling never stopped considering ways in which to improve the efficiency and effectiveness of his command. After the raids in support of the Malta convoy he decided to return to his campaign against the airfields and began to re-equip the units with two elements which were to

24

greatly increase their effectiveness and firepower. Up to now, the SAS had largely relied on the LRDG for transport to and from their battlegrounds; now they began to acquire their own transport, and increase their range of operations. The first element was the American 'General Purpose' vehicle, called the GP or jeep, and the second was the Vickers 'K' air-cooled machine-gun. The jeep, a light, tough, four-wheel-drive vehicle was a war-winner, most useful to the Allied armies, while the Vickers 'K', though designed for aircraft use, gave the SAS a considerable amount of firepower.

Stirling found the Vickers 'K' guns while rooting about in an aircraft hangar. The RAF had no use for them so he took them back to Kabrit and had them fitted to the jeeps, turning a reconnaissance vehicle into a fast and formidable fighting machine. Thus equipped and with his own transport, he flung his raiding net ever wider, establishing forward bases well behind the enemy lines, and using the Vickers 'K' guns to overwhelm airfield defences. This firepower was becoming increasingly necessary. The Germans were intelligent soldiers and after enduring six months of Stirling's attention, they had strengthened their airfield defences to the point at which infiltration raids were becoming difficult and costly; the raiders could usually get in but getting out and away was not so easy. Stirling, therefore, had another idea.

Stirling discovered the usefulness of the Vickers 'K'-armed jeep in action almost by accident, when, accompanied by Paddy Mayne, he had set off to attack two airfields. Stirling stayed at the rendezvous while Mayne put in the attack. Paddy managed to destroy 22 aircraft at Bagush but returned to their rendezvous dejected. 'Some of the fuses didn't go off,' he complained. 'I had to leave about twenty aircraft just sitting there . . . it's tragic.'

Then Stirling had his idea. 'Let's try driving down onto the airfield and shoot them up from the jeeps,' he said. 'These "K" guns are supposed to shoot down aircraft after all, so let's see how they work.' They worked very well.

The garrison were still clearing up the mess which

followed Paddy's visit earlier in the evening, when the SAS erupted once again onto the airfield. The jeeps rolled slowly down the runways, hosing the parked aircraft with machine-gun fire, and had destroyed another twelve before cannon shells began to skip dangerously near the jeeps. Stirling and Paddy were tickled pink by their latest wheeze and decided to put it to use later in a major attack on the bomber airfield at Fuka.

To mount this attack on an airfield well behind the enemy lines, Stirling first established a forward base, 30 miles inland from the coast in an area of deep, dry valleys – or wadis. Jeeps could be concealed in the wadis and supplies of petrol and ammunition built up. It was from this base that Stirling deployed a force of eighteen Vickers 'K'-armed jeeps for the mass assault on Fuka airfield.

This airfield, known as Landing Ground 12, was the main supply airfield for the Afrika Korps. It was in constant use and always full of aircraft. Unlike their normal practice, this time the SAS would attack in full moonlight, with Stirling leading the jeeps in two columns straight across the airfield with every gun firing to the front or flank. Since the risk of shooting each other would be quite considerable, the SAS staged a little night practice on the flat desert above the sheltering wadis, and on the next night they set out across the desert for their target.

The journey took several hours, the jeeps, laden with petrol and ammunition, bumping slowly across the desert, their lights out, the drivers finding their way around obstacles by the light of the moon. Then suddenly, there it was, right before them – Fuka airfield, full of activity, runways lit, aircraft taxiing about, all operations in full swing.

Stirling didn't hesitate. He crashed his jeep directly through the perimeter fence and as an aircraft swept in overhead to land, he followed it down the main runway, the other jeeps at his back. The gunners on Stirling's jeep opened fire; 68 Vickers 'Ks', each loaded with tracer and ball, belched flame behind him, a Guy Fawkes-night riot of colour as the red and green tracers looped away into their targets.

First, to overawe the enemy, the SAS sprayed the airfield with tracer bullets for two full minutes. Then Stirling put up a Very light and, as previously practised, the jeeps slid into two neat columns and proceeded slowly down the main runway, between the rows of parked aircraft, all guns firing into the aircraft as they came into view. The effect was shattering: one by one, the German aircraft burst into flame, exploded, crashed over onto the ground, or burned in a crackle of exploding small-arms ammunition. Flames lit up the sky, providing perfect visibility as the jeeps rolled on and set about their targets.

Finally, after a considerable interval, the startled Germans pulled themselves together and began to fire back. A mortar bomb fell with a thud between the jeep lines, a heavy cannon began to beat from a weapons pit. Stirling's jeep was hit by shell splinters, then another was hit and burst into flames, then a gunner was killed. It was clearly time to withdraw. The SAS jeeps circled the airfield once more, shooting up one last group of parked bombers, and then, as suddenly as they had come, they were gone, leaving behind them nothing but the glow of fires and the steady crackle of burning ammunition.

The 'Great Jeep Attack' took place in July 1942. For the next few months, up to the start of the Battle of Alamein in October, the SAS were continually in action, raiding almost at will along the North African coast. Then, in rapid succession, they suffered two major reverses. The first was an abortive raid on Benghazi, an operation mounted in support of a major assault on Tobruk.

Tobruk was not a small-scale, clandestine operation of the type best suited to the SAS, but a full-scale assault landing, with naval gunfire and air support, the brainchild of another special forces officer, a Colonel Haselden. Haselden proposed a major attack on Rommel's two main ports, Benghazi and Tobruk. Haselden would attack Tobruk and make the main assault while Stirling made a diversionary attack on Benghazi. The SAS were directed to take 40 jeeps full of SAS troopers and commandos into Benghazi, and destroy all the harbour installations, in the hope that this major assault would divert German strength, and in particular German aircraft, from the Allied warships bombarding Tobruk.

Stirling felt the operation to be suicidal. Previous to this he had either planned his own operations or mounted them after discussion with GHQ; now the plans were being taken out of his hands and he was being directed to commit his forces to an operation totally unsuited to their strength and tactics. However, orders being orders he had no choice but to obey. As Stirling expected, the enemy had already obtained intelligence of such a major operation, and the road into Benghazi was blocked, mined and lined with ambushes. After a brief fire-fight outside the town he was forced to withdraw, and in the course of returning across the desert, enemy aircraft destroyed many of his jeeps and killed or captured a quarter of his force.

In the Tobruk attack Haselden's men fared no better. The SIG, who also took part, were decimated and those taken prisoner were, as usual, shot. Haselden was killed and most of his force either killed or captured. As a final bonus, German aircraft sank three of the escort destroyers and several assault craft.

The second reversal, smaller in scale, was more serious for the SAS. In January 1943, while sleeping in a cave behind the German lines, Stirling was captured, accidentally, by a group of Germans on a training exercise; his actual captor was the unit's dentist. Stirling escaped from captivity the same day, but the Arabs he took shelter with betrayed him to the Germans. Rommel himself noted this capture down in his diary: 'We have just captured Colonel Stirling, commander of a force that has caused us considerable trouble in recent months. He was captured by a patrol but later escaped. A tall man, he was soon picked up by the Arabs, who offered him to us for five kilos of tea – a bargain we were glad to accept.'

Stirling spent the rest of the war in captivity, making several attempts to escape and finally ending up in the 'bad boys' prison camp at Castle Colditz. The SAS Regiment he had created and led fought on throughout the war.

3

THE BATTLE FOR THE ISLANDS

To the SAS, Stirling's capture was much more than a personal blow to the men he had recruited and led. Apart from enjoying the benefit of his leadership, the SAS Regiment was very much Stirling's own 'private army'. He was the only person who really knew what was going on and after he disappeared, chaos reigned for some months. New jeeps and stores would arrive but no one knew who they were for; patrols in the field would radio in for fresh orders and no one knew what they were doing out there in the first place. Some patrols even had to be recalled in order to explain their mission. More seriously, the SAS needed to reorganise and find a new field of operations as the Desert War came to a victorious conclusion.

The SAS began to reorganise even before the end of the war in Africa. Stirling's original force, recently called the 1st SAS Regiment, now became the SRS (Special Raiding Squadron) under the command of Paddy Mayne. The 2nd SAS Regiment, under Stirling's brother Bill, had arrived in North Africa and was then under the command of First Army; the Special Boat Section became the Special Boat Service under the command of Earl Jellicoe.

All these three elements of the SAS went on to further exploits in different operational areas, SRS raiding the coasts of Sicily and Italy, 2nd SAS ashore in Italy, and the SBS raiding the islands in the Aegean and the Adriatic. These German-held islands, off the coast of Greece, Yugoslavia and Turkey, became the hunting ground for one of the great fighting soldiers of the war, a man to rival the already legendary Paddy Mayne – the redoubtable Dane, Anders Lassen.

Like so many of the wartime SAS, Lt Anders Lassen was a 'character'. He had a penchant for collecting odorous and scruffy dogs, he believed that the bow and arrow was a useful weapon of modern war, and he had a very low boredom threshold. However senior the officer in charge, Lassen would simply walk out of any briefing which became tedious, crashing out the door, throwing a curt 'I go now' over his shoulder.

Once in action though, Lassen was a man who mattered. Between April 1943 and his death at Lake Commachio in Italy in 1945, he killed or captured more enemy soldiers than anyone else in the Eastern Mediterranean. Lassen became one of the leading lights of the SBS which based itself at Athlit, in what is now Israel, in April 1943 and began to create fresh problems for the enemy then occupying the scattered islands of Greece.

In June 1943 the SBS mounted their first independent raid on Crete, which Jellicoe and Berge had raided under Stirling's direction the year before. Lassen led one of the three four-man patrols to the island and attacked the airfield at Kastelli which, being full of Junkers and Stuka aircraft, was heavily guarded. Lassen decided to divert the guards while the rest of his party attacked the aircraft.

Getting through the sentries, Lassen began to shake the place up with grenades and bursts of tommy-gun fire – keeping this up until the garrison was in a panic and the aircraft started to explode. Ignoring the men attacking the aircraft, the guards chased Lassen up into the hills, where he hid without food and water for three days before he could rejoin the rest of his party and return to the coast.

There was an amusing aftermath. The patrol had captured two German soldiers on the airfield and, passing through Cairo after getting back to Egypt, the party felt thirsty and decided to stop for a drink at Groppis, the social centre of the city. Since no one wanted to guard the prisoners, the SBS took them into the bar as well and stood them a cold beer, nobody appearing to notice the German uniforms among the rest.

Having cut their teeth in Crete, the SBS then turned their attention to the island of Rhodes, the largest island in the Dodecanese and one held by a large garrison of Italians. Italy was on the point of surrendering to the Allies and the main SBS objective on Rhodes was to stiffen the Italian troops and make them fight against their former Allies when the Germans sent troops to occupy the island. The Italian commander, Admiral Campione, was none too pleased at being sandwiched between 10,000 tough German troops and the even tougher, if much fewer, SBS soldiers. He therefore sat firmly on the fence, until the Germans lost their patience and attacked Rhodes Town in force.

The Italians put up a feeble resistance, but after harrassing the invaders for some days, the SBS withdrew in comfort, complete with picnic baskets and bottles of wine, to the nearby island of Castelrosso, from where they proceeded to take over the other islands of the Dodecanese. Jellicoe occupied Castelrosso, Kos and Leros with only 80 men and held them, on and off, for months, only withdrawing when the Germans arrived in force, and returning to recapture them when SBS raids diverted German troops elsewhere. The SBS ranged these islands in small boats, Greek schooners (or caiques), MTBs, even canoes, and no place was spared their attention.

Even when captured, the SBS managed to make a nuisance of themselves. Take, for example, the doings of Private Watler. Captured by the Germans on Kos, and confined in the Crusader castle, he escaped over the walls the same night using a length of electric cable as a rope. Six hours later he was recaptured (Kos is a very small place), and two days later escaped yet again. Deciding to avoid the land this time, he went to the beach and swam down the coast, coming ashore from time to time to empty German petrol drums piled on the jetties by driving nails into them. He later rejoined his unit and fought on throughout the war.

Having captured Kos, the Germans turned their attention to Simi. Here the SBS determined to oppose the German landing with the aid of the Italian garrison. This 'aid' was achieved by Anders Lassen standing behind the Italian commander, holding a pistol at his back, and 'urging' his men to resist. The German force landed at dawn from two Greek schooners, and the SBS garrison, under Captain Lapraik, engaged them at once with machine-gun fire. The Germans got ashore but were quickly boxed in on the beaches and in Simi town, where they began to suffer severe casualties from SBS snipers. With Lassen 'encouraging' the Italians to counter-attack, the Germans eventually withdrew in disorder, though they then turned their attention to Leros, which British forces had already garrisoned in some strength. The SBS hurried over to join them and await the German onslaught, which eventually began on 12 November 1943 with a parachute landing and air attacks. Leros fell after days of heavy fighting, but once again the SBS slipped away before the final surrender, to lie up on the nearby island of Lisso before withdrawing to regroup on the mainland of Turkey. Here they were joined some days later by one of their number, Lt Keith Balsillie, who had escaped from captivity on Leros, stolen a boat and rowed it across to Turkey.

If the Germans thought that occupying all the islands had removed the risk of SAS/SBS attacks, they were quite wrong. They had simply provided the SBS with more targets, and now that the Germans had occupied all the islands of the Dodecanese and removed the Italians, the area was wide open for more SBS raids. The Germans had to garrison all the islands, but none could be held in any strength, and the SBS soon began to prey on these scattered forces. Take, for another example, a typical night on Simi, during the visit of an SBS patrol, led by Lt Bob Bury.

The Simi garrison consisted of about 90 assorted German soldiers. The SBS patrol arrived at the southern end of the island, near the Governor's House, the German headquarters, where a large window was conveniently open, giving the raiders access to the first floor, which they duly entered. A bomb had caused some damage to the interior of this part of the house and progress inside was therefore slow and not entirely silent. Hearing voices coming from the ground floor, Bury investigated and found a German light machine-gun post. He threw a grenade inside the room which stopped all conversation.

Hearing other Germans on the quay outside discussing the explosion, his colleague Sergeant Geary investigated. Geary saw a group of seven Germans standing about, into whom he fired a full magazine of Schmeisser bullets from 30 yards range. Three men fell immediately; the others rushed into the house but were all killed by another burst of fire.

While this was going on Bob Bury, now out in the street, was taking a look in a window of the house next door. Here he spotted another German, whom he shot with his carbine. He then detonated a 25 lb explosive charge on the ground floor and when the building collapsed, part of the Governor's House went with it. Before retreating Bury and his patrol left a 10 lb pack of explosive in the street behind them, which some pursuing Italian Fascists tried to neutralise. The resulting explosion blew them to pieces.

Lassen went to Calchi and discovered, according to the mayor, that there were 'only six Fascists on the whole island'. Lassen felt that this made it scarcely worth the journey, but he continued to the police station and ordered those within to open up. When they refused, Lassen broke down the door, took the Italians prisoner and confiscated such useful items as a number of typewriters, a shotgun, the rifles, a radio receiver, two Beretta machine-carbines and the telephone. He also noticed the office safe and was about to blow it open when he heard the sound of an approaching motorboat. An armed German launch, belonging to the flotilla based on Rhodes, was coming into the harbour. Lassen hid his men by the quay and opened fire on the launch at close range. Two Germans out of the six on board were wounded and the remaining four surrendered at once. Lassen added the motorboat and its stores, which included four live pigs, to his booty and returned with it in triumph to Turkey. There was only one British casualty: Lassen himself was slightly injured, shot in the foot by a bullet from one of his own men.

SBS operations were often like this; small, quixotic and effective, using surprise, firepower and training to overcome the enemy, who could never know from where, or in what force, the next attack was coming. SBS operations tied down thousands of German troops and gave great support to the resistance fighters and partisans of Greece and Yugoslavia.

Even in their stronghold at Rhodes, the Germans were not safe. Jellicoe's second-in-command, Major Ian Patterson, learned that the German garrison on Rhodes were sending a detachment to remove all the children from the orphanage on nearby Nisiros. Patterson contacted the Mother Superior and asked her to take the children to safety at the top of a nearby mountain. Then he placed his men at strategic points within and around the orphanage and, disguising himself, for some reason, as an Italian priest, awaited the arrival of the Germans.

Later that day, Major Patterson saw a German party coming up the road towards the orphanage. He met the visitors, led them along a passage to the orphanage refectory, and asked them to wait there while he assembled the children. The SBS then took up their positions in front of the orphanage while Patterson doubled back behind his men and took up a position at the rear of the building.

While the SBS were taking up these positions, the Germans became suspicious and opened fire through the windows at the surrounding troops. Fortunately, the SBS had been well trained at close-quarter fighting, while the Germans had not. Their shooting was well off the mark as a gun battle raged through the various rooms of the orphanage. At one moment, Major Patterson was seized by a German soldier, but Lt-Commander Ramsaur, a naval officer with little experience of using a pistol, then rushed up from behind and blew the German's brains out. Not one German escaped, and the few who leapt through the windows were caught by the soldiers posted outside.

However, even after those at the orphanage had been subdued, there were other Germans down at the harbour, who would certainly become suspicious if their comrades did not return. Patterson took a group of men armed with a Bren gun and Lewes bombs, who worked their way unseen up a hill until they could position the Bren within easy range of the German ship. The Germans were taking it easy on deck, evidently still unaware of events at the orphanage. Patterson and his men arrived just in time though, for two Germans, sent from the ship to investigate the delay at the orphanage, rushed back to sound the alarm. Patterson promptly opened fire with the Bren and sprayed the contents of several magazines over the open target below his position.

Lt Dick Harden, with Corporal Long and Lance-Corporal Clark, both Royal Marines, were hidden only 150 yards from the quayside. Under cover of the Bren gun fire, they rushed forward and engaged the Germans at close range with their carbines and grenades. Retaliation by the Germans was neutralised by Patterson and Harden, throwing 1 lb primed charges of plastic high explosive onto the deck. The Germans surrendered with the exception of the officer, who blamed his defeat by a much smaller force on 'the black treachery of the Greeks'.

Patterson then made plans for departure. He left the Germans who were seriously wounded and requiring immediate medical attention in the care of the nuns at the orphanage. Then, after acknowledging the congratulations of the mayor and other local dignitaries, he set out for Turkey. Almost 40 tons of food supplies, destined for the garrison of Kos, were discovered on the German boat, together with live pigs and a stock of wine and brandy which was shared between the SBS and the local population.

Exactly how the SBS were able to operate from bases in supposedly neutral Turkey has never been clearly explained, but in the space of a few weeks, the SBS had turned the previously quiet islands of the Dodecanese into a front-line fighting zone. Matters worsened for the German garrisons when Lassen returned from hospital and took a hand in the game, leading his patrol to attack the island of Santorini.

On the first floor of the bank of Athens in Santorini Town, 48 Italians and twenty Germans occupied a billet. Lassen, taking with him his close friend, a Greek officer, Stefan Casulli, and twelve men, managed to surprise the enemy, despite many sentries and police dogs patrolling the town. Once inside the billet they set out to slaughter the garrison, racing from room to room with pistol and grenades. He and Sergeant Nicholson had a well-established routine. Nicholson would kick the door open, then Lassen would throw in two grenades. Then Nicholson, firing his Bren from the hip, would spray around the walls and corners. Finally, Lassen would clear the room with his pistol. Only a handful of the enemy survived this swoop. But Stefan Casulli was also killed, shot in the chest, and Casulli's room-clearing companion, Sergeant Kingston, died from a wound in the stomach the following day.

Santorini is a crescent-shaped volcanic island, with very little cover, and had the defending ground forces not been virtually demoralised, events might have gone badly for Lassen on the next day. Fortunately, the enemy headquarters on the larger island of Melos believed that the island had been captured and did not appear with reinforcements for over 48 hours, during which time Lassen was able to collect his scattered forces and leave without trouble. The Germans gave Casulli and Kingston a funeral with full military honours, but on the same day issued a proclamation demanding the names of those who had helped the British commandos. To prevent a massacre the mayor and five others came forward, and were promptly shot.

While raiding widely across the Aegean, the SBS never forgot their withdrawal from Simi on October 1943, and Captain Lapraik for one, was determined to recapture it.

The Simi operation had been under consideration for some time, but it never looked a practical possibility as long as the enemy had naval forces, including destroyers, in the Aegean. Destroyers could prevent landing operations or attack the SBS as they withdrew in caiques. At the beginning of 1944 there had been four German destroyers in the Eastern Mediterranean, and although the German navy seldom put to sea, their presence kept the SBS at bay.

In March, one of the ships was damaged by a British submarine and later a second took a bomb amidships from a Beaufighter. There remained two, in Leros. To cope with these, Brigadier Turnbull asked London to let him have a small party of canoe raiders from the Royal Marine Boom Commando, the forerunners of the Royal Marines Special Boat Section of modern times. This unit had already attacked German shipping in the Gironde and was well suited to raiding warships in harbour. When the Royal Marines first arrived in the Middle East their dress and drill drew tart remarks from the rather ragamuffin SBS, but this attitude quickly changed when it was seen that the newcomers could handle their frail craft with great precision. In mid-June the Marines paddled into Leros harbour, crossed two booms, and sank the surviving destroyers at their moorings – retiring without loss.

On 6 July, therefore, Stewart Macbeth returned to the SBS base. He had undertaken a reconnaissance of Simi and knew the enemy positions intimately. Two days later the full strike force, under Brigadier Turnbull, who commanded all SAS raiders in the Aegean, comprising twelve ships, 81 SBS and 139 men from the Greek Sacred Squadron, was concentrated under camouflage in Turkey. Three separate parties were formed: the main force under the brigadier with Lapraik as his deputy; west force under Captain Charles Clynes; and south force under Macbeth. On the night of 13 July they landed unobserved on Simi, the only casualties being two Greek officers who fell into the water carrying heavy packs and drowned.

Before dawn all forces were lying up, overlooking their

targets. As soon as it was light the main enemy stronghold by the harbour was attacked with mortar fire and machine-guns. Two German barges, which had left harbour a short time before, came hurrying back, having sighted the five armed British launches sailing towards the port. The SBS opened fire on these ships and before long flags could be seen waving from their bridges.

Meanwhile, another SBS officer, 'Stud' Stellin, was attacking the German positions on Molo Point. He had taken the first objective without opposition, but before he could consolidate his gains, German soldiers came running up the hill to man their machine-guns. Stellin opened up with his carbine, which jammed. He called upon his 'oppo' Private Whalen, to '. . . give them the works' with a Bren. The two then went down on the enemy with grenades and soon all were either dead, wounded or surrendering. Stellin locked the prisoners in Simi church, posted a sentry outside and moved on to his next objective, the caique yards in the harbour below the castle at Simi Town.

Three hours after the attack began, main force, with the Vickers machine-gun and mortar troops, had advanced to within 800 yards of the castle. Fire centred on this from all angles, with mortar bombs exploding on the battlements and a tracer racing through every opening. The enemy was putting up a tough fight and keeping up a steady fire, mainly aimed at Stellin's men. While crossing a bridge, three of Stellin's troops became pinned down under the low parapet, the slightest movement drawing enemy fire on them. Stellin told them to stay where they were, and unable to get out, there they stayed, smoking cigarettes, until the castle surrendered three hours later. South force, under Macbeth and Bob Bury, had attacked a German position in a monastery. This they swiftly overcame and drove the survivors down a promontory towards the tip of the island, where Macbeth sent them a note calling upon them to surrender. The first demand was rejected by the enemy as unreadable. It was then rewritten with the aid of a young local girl, who volunteered to carry it through the lines, after which 33 of the enemy promptly surrendered.

With all three of the SBS groups now engaged, the fight for Simi was getting into its stride. Around the castle the SBS mortar fire had caused the enemy many casualties and much discomfort, but not sufficient to bring about their surrender. It was considered that the position could not be taken by direct assault, so the SBS decided to consolidate, make the maximum display of strength and offer surrender terms to the enemy.

Brigadier Turnbull sent a captured German petty officer up to the castle under escort, with orders to inform the enemy that they were completely surrounded, that the rest of the island was in British hands, and that further resistance on their part was useless. The petty officer returned within the hour and declared that the enemy were prepared to talk. Lieutenant Kenneth Fox of the SBS, who spoke fluent German, then returned to the castle with the petty officer and a further hour went by, during which the only incident was the emergence of a party of Italian *carabinieri* from the castle, their leader waving a Red Cross flag. Lt-Commander Ramsaur, the naval officer who had somehow become attached to the SBS, was then sent in to hurry things along and found Fox and the German commander deep in conference. At last the surrender was arranged and the garrison duly marched out. They were barely out of the castle when three Messerschmitts flew over the port and dropped anti-personnel bombs. 'You see, that's what comes of being late,' remarked the German commander. 'I thought they had forgotten us because I radioed for air support several hours ago.'

The battle being over, friends and foes took tea in the boat yards, while sausages were fried and an ox roasted by the delighted population. The prisoners were relieved to find themselves well treated instead of being shot, and they revealed the whereabouts of the wine stocks in their living quarters. Bottles were quickly transferred to the SBS craft, to be drunk back at base. Meanwhile, Lapraik, Macbeth and Stellin, who were already well known on the island, were being welcomed at the town hall and congratulated by the mayor.

At midnight most of the force sailed, taking the prisoners with them. Stellin and his patrol remained behind as rear party, with orders from headquarters to report subsequent events on Simi and to distribute the 30 tons of food which the SBS had brought in for the half-starved civilian population. The SBS were also concerned that their raid might result, as elsewhere, in German reprisals against the civilian population.

The Germans retaliated in another way. Next day the town, with its defenceless population, was heavily bombed. Stellin and his men came out when it was over to find two enemy motor launches entering the harbour. When they opened fire the ships withdrew in flames, but more bombers approached and the SBS withdrew rapidly to one of the more remote mountains, from which point they watched the German flag being hoisted once again over Simi Town.

That night, while embarking on a launch, they encountered a patrolling 'E' boat. Fortunately Stellin's patrol had captured many automatic weapons and was thus armed strongly enough to make battle. The 'E' boat was left sinking by the beach as the SBS slipped away, back to their hiding place in Turkey.

4

THE PARTISAN WAR

The Simi raid marked the end of SBS operations in the
Aegean. The Greek Sacred Squadron, well trained in SAS
techniques, took over here in their home area and Lapraik
was able to write to the Greek commander: 'Your group
will operate in the Aegean until further notice. For the
present, you will confine yourself to reconnaissance, but
in September, raiding activities will be resumed upon a
much larger scale.' The operations of the Sacred Squadron must, however, remain another story, while we follow
the SBS to the coast of Yugoslavia and into the 'big war'
on the Italian mainland. Before leaving, though, it is
worth taking another look at the intrepid Dane.

Anders Lassen had by now been promoted to Major, and
while the rest of the SBS were regrouping for raids in
Yugoslavia, he continued to harry the retreating Germans in
the offshore islands of Greece. On 22 October he embarked
40 men in two motor launches and proceeded towards the
islands of the Sporades, on a voyage that offered them little
action but much comedy. He called first at Skopelos and
found that it had been recently evacuated by the enemy. He
then decided to try Skiathos, and was about to land on that
island, which was unoccupied, when another motor launch,
carrying members of Brigadier Turnbull's raiding forces,
approached and demanded to know what they were up to.
A short discussion followed and it was decided, rank having
certain privileges, that representatives of Brigadier Turnbull
should land a few minutes in advance of Lassen's party.

It was discovered that the enemy had just left Volos on the nearby mainland, abandoning a number of schooners and a merchant ship in the harbour. However, in order to make their departure felt, the Germans shelled Skiathos harbour from long distance. While this was proceeding, the British party were approached by an unknown British major. 'Hello, sailors,' he said. 'Just the fellows I want to see. I've got ten thousand Italians I want you to take off my hands at once. When can you embark them?'

The SBS pointed to their tiny craft and said that they could manage four if that would help. The major had fed, clothed and hidden these Italians since the armistice with Italy a year before. Asked if he spoke Italian, the major replied, 'Good God, no, old boy. I'm a sapper.' Odd things like that happened all over the Eastern Mediterranean.

Lt Bob Bury had also been diverted for coastal reconnaissance. His patrol was approaching a large bay, known to be held by guerrillas. 'From what we learnt later,' wrote his sergeant, 'the partisans were expecting an attack by their deadly enemies, the Communist ELAS. When we sailed in they opened fire upon us.' The helmsman was hit, so Bury jumped up and took his place, but had no means of making his identity known except by shouting. He steered a course which would bring him close to the guns but was unable to take cover, and while doing this he was fatally wounded. Bury was 24 years old when he died, and had spent all his adult life in warfare. He was buried the following day by the men who had killed him in error.

Lassen was becoming bored with unoccupied islands and set off for a reconnaissance of Salonika on the Greek mainland, embarking his latest toy, a new jeep, on a small schooner, escorted for part of the way by two motor launches. The area close to the city of Salonika was occupied by the enemy but Lassen's schooner, concealed among a fleet of harmless Greek shipping, attracted no attention and through binoculars he was able to watch the retreating Germans evacuating gun positions two miles away.

In fact, it was the forces of the Greek Communist Party, ELAS, and not the Germans who were in control of the coastline and hinterland. Their commander instructed his men to be as unhelpful as possible to the Allied soldiers – an unwise course to take with a man like Lassen, who so harrassed him that he soon threw up his command and disappeared from the scene.

The opposing forces, German and ELAS, though in many instances only a few hundred yards apart, showed reluctance to fight. When the Germans left an area, ELAS simply moved into it and declared that the area had been liberated; a peaceful process that left German strength intact and gave much propaganda advantage to the Communists, who were hoping to seize control of Greece after the war.

Lassen, however, impressed the partisans so much that their attitude soon changed considerably. At first the local people, thinking that the British were Germans, would run frightened back into their houses and children would run away in terror. But when they realised the British had finally arrived the excitement was incredible, and the SBS advance became a mixture of fighting and celebrations.

Meanwhile, Martin Solomon, a naval liaison officer attached to the SAS and an old pal of Lassen, had left for another coastal reconnaissance of a gun battery which the Germans were reputed to be evacuating. He was accompanied by Lieutenant Henshaw, a guardsman who was usually Lassen's second-in-command. The battery was still in existence, but due for removal the next day, so having ambushed a truck carrying supplies, the SBS decided to trick the Germans into surrender. Henshaw, who spoke good German, wrote a note to the enemy commander informing him that he was completely surrounded by British troops and might as well give up immediately, unless of course he preferred to be starved and attacked.

This note was duly despatched and while waiting for the reply, Henshaw and Solomon were joined by two German soldiers who had been drinking and who mistook them for comrades. The Germans were taken prisoner, but while the four were discussing events, Henshaw and Solomon saw two tanks, six self-propelled guns, and six lorry-loads of troops approaching. The battery commander had decided to fight. The two men abandoned their jeep, and taking their prisoners with them, made a hurried escape.

When they had time to stop and think, the magnitude of what they had just done dawned upon them. The thought of what Lassen would do to them for the loss of his beloved jeep far outweighed anything which the Germans could do. After a cold night spent in a wood, Henshaw crept down to the battery at dawn and found the jeep still intact 100 yards away from where the Germans were demolishing their emplacements. Under cover of their explosions he drove the vehicle away. Once back at base, Lassen listened to their story with interest. 'You have done well,' he said, but commented, 'Had you not brought the jeep back, I would have slit your throats.' They almost believed him.

The German front in Greece was crumbling and the retreat was now in earnest. With his unique genius for the unusual, Lassen commandeered four fire engines for the entry of the SBS into Salonika. When it was found that the western half of the town was still defended, the ELAS forces were happy to call a halt. Lassen, however, declaring that Allied prestige must be maintained, drove on to the attack. In the distance, explosions could be heard as German engineers demolished the petrol installations. Reaching the German lines, the fire engines screamed to a halt. Greek citizens, who had leapt aboard in the excitement of liberation, hastily dashed for cover and the SBS opened fire. The German rearguard had no proper protection and were without leaders, so the fight was soon over, with over 60 enemy casualties, while the SBS did not lose a man. When they returned in triumph to the city centre, many of the red flags which had been hung out to celebrate the liberation of Salonika were gone, having been replaced in the meantime by Union Jacks.

This may all sound like fun, but what was the point of

it if the enemy were already in full retreat? According to one high-ranking officer, 'But for Lassen and his men, Salonika would not have been evacuated as soon as October 1944 and the town would have suffered even greater destruction. His solitary jeep and few troops were seen everywhere; behind the enemy's lines, with ELAS, and up in the mountains. Their numbers and strength were magnified into many hundreds of men; rifles and pistols into automatic weapons. Prisoners taken confirmed this and their estimate of SBS strength was never less than one thousand men.' The war in the Greek islands was coming to a close and it is time to follow Anders Lassen and his band of brothers to the mainland of Italy.

Andy Lassen always wanted to see what he called the 'big war' and as usual he finally got his way. Normally Lassen and his squadron would have taken over the island operations off the coast of Yugoslavia, but when these islands began to capitulate, the way became clear for a move which he had long planned, and in which he was assisted by Brigadier Ronald Tod of the 2nd Special Service Brigade, which was now in action on the Italian mainland.

After the capture of the Gothic Line in the autumn of 1944, the Eighth Army had at last entered upon the plain of Bologna. They had then, with some difficulty, captured Forli, Ravenna and Faenza but had been unable to penetrate further, for the Lower Romagna is a flat and marshy plain with dykes, canals and small rivers intersecting the marshes. It is a breeding ground for mosquitoes, and a far from pleasant place, beginning below Argenta and ending in the many false shorelines of the Adriatic. The front line ran from Lake Commachio on the coast along the river Senio to Castel Bolognese and the main route, Highway 12, of which we shall be hearing more. It was on this bleak front that the tired troops of the Eighth Army – Poles, British, New Zealanders, even a Jewish brigade – spent the last cold winter of the war. Patrols and outposts dug themselves in behind the steep banks of the rivers and canals and the main forces watched each other from a discreet distance.

Brigadier Tod and his force, which comprised No. 2 and No. 9 Army Commandos and two Royal Marine Commandos, held the extreme right flank of the line. In front of them lay Lake Commachio and, between the sea and the Commachio lagoon, ran a stretch of scrub-covered sand dunes which the Germans had fortified and mined. If a landing could be made behind, from across the lake, the German fortifications would surely fall and the main position in the Bologna plain to the west would be outflanked. This operation was therefore considered to be vital to Field-Marshal Alexander's spring offensive and it was to be carried out as soon as possible by the commando brigade in co-operation with SBS.

Lake Commachio is a vast flooded area rather than a proper lake. Even at the centre it is fairly shallow and children could have paddled out for miles were it not for the danger of being sucked down by the mud. From the shore, Commachio looks like a normal stretch of water, but the average depth is only two feet, except in the middle and in certain channels, where it is very slightly deeper. Few of these channels were charted and there was no reason why they should have been, for Commachio had hardly any fish and contained few islands. It was a considerable military obstacle – too shallow for large assault craft, too large to be splashed across, too boggy for tanks. The few small islands in the lake were wooded and held ruined houses which were used by the Germans as observation points for artillery.

The problems of transporting large numbers of heavily laden men across four miles of such a lake were considerable, since only a fraction of the shore was in British hands. The northern, western and eastern shores were held by the Germans, who possessed a clear field of fire. Only on the south was there a strip of commando-held territory, on the high banks of the river Senio, just where it entered the lake. From the opposite side of the river German sentries lay watching.

Lassen and his men moved up to Ravenna by truck at the end of March, carrying with them folding canoes,

Goatley assault craft and rubber boats. Lassen brought with him his collection of scruffy dogs, his German army Volkswagen, his cooks and many Italian camp followers who had joined him at intervals along the way. Installed in moderate conditions of comfort at Ravenna, Lassen went out in his jeep to inspect the area of operations and to interview his superior officers on their intentions. When Lassen was satisfied, operations began. The SBS task was to find a way across for the main commando force, infiltrate the enemy positions and, in effect, 'hold the bridge' until reinforcements could arrive.

Silence and surprise were essential: it was important that the German observers were not alarmed by any unusual movement or the sound of motor engines, so every man who crossed the lake had to paddle until the very last moment. This they had to do in their Goatleys, canoes, rubber life-rafts or other types of craft normally reserved for the shipwrecked. Anything less like the meticulously equipped Normandy landings cannot be imagined.

Every night during the first week of April Lassen went out on the lake, stealing about softly in the dark, until the blank large-scale map of the area in Brigadier Tod's headquarters became covered with notes and diagrams of routes and canals, each charted by Lassen's soldiers. When the main attack finally took place, he and his squadron would lead the assault, guiding the commando force through the deeper channels with lights and flares.

The big attack across Commachio took place on 9 April. Lassen's methods for signalling the assault craft across were completely successful and a strip of land on the north shore was cleared to a depth of over four miles after heavy fighting.

During the development of the main attack, Lassen's force had been ordered to make a diversion on the northern shore of Commachio. For the job he chose Lt Turnbull, but at the last moment decided to go along with this officer himself. Lassen's old 'oppo', Guardsman O'Reilly, with Sergeant Waite and his patrol made up the remainder of the party. They landed on the enemy shore and

47

advanced along a road well defended by pill-boxes. Heavy machine-gun fire was soon opened up on the patrol and O'Reilly was seriously wounded. The rest took cover in the lake, dragging O'Reilly with them, but Lassen continued to advance, attacking and destroying the machine-gun post and then the first pill-box with grenades. Then he went on, with pistol and grenades, to get a second pill-box, a third and a fourth in the same way, shooting down anyone who got in his way. The fifth pill-box along the road showed a white flag, but as Lassen advanced to take the surrender he was shot at close range.

He did not die at once, but managed to crawl back towards his own men who came running forward to complete the work he had almost finished single-handed. When they returned to him he was still alive.

'Leave me,' he ordered, 'I'm done for.' They carried him back until, coming under heavy machine-gun fire and finding his body lifeless, they were forced to leave him. Lassen was just 25 years old when he died, only one month before the end of the war in Europe.

There was at the time an unwritten rule that the Victoria Cross cannot be awarded to two men in the same battle, and a Victoria Cross was won that night by a corporal in a Royal Marine Commando. Lassen's case called for an exception, so a second recommendation for the Victoria Cross was put forward and this was successful. Lassen became the second foreigner, and the second Dane, to win the Victoria Cross.

The battles for the islands, and at Commachio, were unusual, even for the SAS, but they marked another step in the story of the regiment. Raiding from the sea, 'hearts and minds' with the long-suffering civilian population, political problems with the Italian Fascists and Greek Communists, the art of deception, and finally infiltration before a main assault, were all added to the growing list of regimental skills. In the future, on different fronts, against other enemies, these skills would be needed again.

5

THE SAS IN ITALY 1943–4

While the SBS and Anders Lassen were having the time of their lives in Greece, the two other SAS formations, 1 SAS, which for a brief period had been called the Special Raiding Squadron (SRS), and 2 SAS, under Bill Stirling, had carried the war into Italy, where the terrain could hardly have been more different from the open deserts of North Africa. Italy is a rocky, forested, mountainous country, and, in spite of its sun-kissed summer image, prone to long, hard winters when the mountains are deep in snow and the roads along the valley floors collapse into mud. Terrain often dictates tactics and the military situation in Italy was complicated by the fact that in September 1943 the Italians surrendered. The Germans then occupied the country, after which many Italians, notably those with Communist leanings, took to the hills as guerrillas. It was these guerrilla bands that the SAS organised or co-operated with in their deep penetrations behind the enemy lines. SAS operations in Italy began, however, in a more conventional way with seaborne landings at Marro di Porco in Sicily and against the port of Termoli on the mainland of Italy.

SAS tactics are not designed for assault operations from the sea. That role is more suited to their colleagues in the commandos. But the first SAS operation in Italy was a raid in support of the seaborne landings, when a small party of SRS captured three gun batteries at Marro di Porco, killed scores of enemy troops and took over 500 prisoners for the loss of one SRS man killed and a handful of wounded. Once Sicily had been captured, after a five-week campaign, elements of 2 SAS under Major Roy Farran landed at Taranto and then joined up with 1 SAS, led by Paddy Mayne, No. 3 Commando and No. 40 (Royal Marine) Commando for a swift seaborne assault against the road and rail junctions at the town of Termoli on the mainland – an assault which soon developed into a bitter battle with the lightly armed British special force troops fighting German heavy infantry, paratroopers and tanks.

The initial assault on Termoli went well, the town was occupied and all was quiet for the day. Then, the ever-resourceful Germans counter-attacked. Shells began to crash down on the town, several landing in the street and wounding a number of civilians. As the day wore on the weight of this bombardment increased, indicating that an infantry attack was coming, spearheaded by the formidable 16 Panzer Division, which had been ordered to re-take Termoli 'at all costs'.

Regular British infantry of 78 Division arrived in Termoli that evening with several tanks, but several times during the day, pairs of Focke-Wulfs swooped in to bomb the shipping in the harbour. The bombardment became even more intense the next morning, so Farran sent off an officer to see if he could gain news of the situation from the nearby infantry brigade. The officer returned around midday, after a hazardous drive through shell-fire, to tell the story of his meeting with the infantry brigadier. The brigadier, a rather pompous man, had just said, 'Don't worry, old boy! Everything is perfectly under control,' when a German Spandau began to fire at close range into brigade headquarters, forcing the brigadier to dive under an armoured car. Farran did not feel that the situation was at all under control. 78 Division was fighting off fierce German counter-attacks at the bridge, and the commando brigade was soon called back into the line to hold Termoli town.

During the afternoon, when the bombardment was reaching a new peak, Farran gathered together twenty men of 2 SAS with six Bren guns and made his way to the commando brigade headquarters. Their first hour was spent in the cellar beneath HQ, where the staff captain had been killed by a shell only minutes before. German tanks had now reached the edge of the railway line and had overrun the commandos' forward positions. The commandos nevertheless held their ground although surrounded on three sides and under attack by both a Panzer and an infantry division. With the defenders outgunned and outnumbered the situation in Termoli was critical.

Farran's men took up a position on the second-floor balcony of brigade headquarters and, after engaging the advancing enemy from there, moved to take up a fresh position in the railway goods yard. Taking his full force of only twenty men, Farran then moved again to the crest of a hill at right angles to the coast, a mile north of the town. Soon the Germans began to advance on their left flank, which forced Farran's men to fall back on the last ridge before the goods yard. Thanks to the Brens, their fire power was quite abnormally strong for such a small group and Farran was able to cover the front between 1 SAS and the sea by placing ten men with three Brens on each side of the railway line. Their main problem was that they had no tools with which to dig weapon pits, but in spite of heavy fire from the nearby cemetery, the SAS group held this position for three days. Mortar bombs crashed down on them all the time, and crossing the railway from one side of the position to the other was always highly dangerous, with a sniper's bullets cracking past their heads as they ran across the track. Even worse, after they had been in this position for over a day, they discovered that the railway trucks on the line beside them were loaded with high explosive.

Apart from the constant harrassing fire, they were short of rations and the nights were bitter. At last, on the third day, an Irish infantry brigade landed in the harbour and the London Irish moved up to join Farran's men for a counter-attack. The SAS decided to expend their remaining ammunition down the railway line, while the Irish brigade swept in on the German flank from the left. Only when the Germans stood up and began to retreat did the SAS realise how strong their opposition had been. Hundreds of figures in field-grey uniforms began to run back down the line, away from the front, and 1 SAS had stopped a force several score times their strength and held their position until relieved, another well-earned battle honour.

Such exploits, although proving that the SAS trooper is first and foremost a good soldier, were not typical of SAS operations in Italy. To look at these we have to follow the fortunes of Roy Farran, a cavalryman who had joined the SAS at the end of the North African campaign, and was to serve with them until the end of the war, developing a considerable reputation in the process. Farran also persuaded Colonel Grant Taylor, an expert in close-quarter combat with the pistol, to teach his unique skills to the SAS troopers, until most men could put six shots into a playing card at twenty paces. This skill, too, joined the SAS repertoire.

Farran followed his experiences at Termoli by a more typical, if no less hazardous SAS raid, leading a party of sixteen men to attack the central railway line. They landed by boat near Pescara. The landing went according to plan and during the next day they prepared their charges for the attack. The original plan called for the party to lay mines on the road and to blow down telegraph poles, while other parties blew up the tracks along the railway line, but Farran discovered that they were short of explosives as he had drawn a pack full of mines. One wonders why this had not been checked before they sailed.

At ten o'clock on a wild, wet night, they left their position and plodded down the road towards the railway. The rest of the party (which had dispersed after landing) were there on time and they moved off together to the attack, with the rain driving hard into their faces as they crossed the fields, crawling over ditches and scrambling through hedges. Finally they clambered up the wet, grassy bank to the railway, dumped their rucksacks and set about laying their charges. When all was ready, they squeezed the time pencils, picked up their packs and slid down the muddy embankment to the fence below. Soon they were scrambling up muddy paths into the hills, but their rubber boot-soles would not grip the mud and they often slid back down to the bottom of a slope after having struggled to reach the top. The withdrawal became a nightmare, as weighed down by their packs they frequently found themselves crawling along on hands and knees. There was, however, some compensation, for on reaching the top of a particularly difficult ascent, they heard the sound of the explosions far behind and saw distant flashes through the rain. They had blown the main railway line in sixteen places, demolished telegraph poles over a long stretch and blown down an electricity pylon, effectively cutting off local communications for several days.

It was now necessary to get away, and since the Germans had taken to shooting captured SAS soldiers, this was a stage of the operation which demanded as much attention as the approach and the attack. Their retreat through a heavily-occupied and thoroughly aroused countryside took five nights, during which the party was attacked several times, some were taken prisoner and others fell ill with malaria, picked up in the desert. They collected at the embarkation beach on the fifth evening, leaving a party positioned to watch the road behind, with orders to lay Farran's mines across it just before leaving for the boat. They started to signal out to sea by flashing a torch at eleven o'clock, while searching German half-tracks rumbled past along the road behind.

It was almost midnight when they saw the outline of a vessel offshore. It could have been a German E-boat, so they hid themselves in the sand dunes, anticipating a hail of machine-gun fire. Then they saw a rubber boat coming in through the waves. The dinghies made several trips to lift them out, and soon they were all aboard and on their way to safety at their base in Termoli.

Early in the spring of 1944, most of the SAS unit were withdrawn to England to prepare for the D-Day landings in Normandy. Those desert veterans of L Detachment and 1 SAS who trickled into the SAS depot near Prestwick were very surprised to find how fast and how large the SAS had grown. The entire SAS force assembled in Prestwick, and consisted of 1 and 2 SAS, two French SAS Regiments, and a Belgian SAS company, plus various support arms with scores of jeeps and vast amounts of equipment. All this was designated for D-Day and it seemed a far cry from Kabrit. The SAS exploits in France must wait for the next chapter, for we have not yet finished with Italy.

Roy Farran's squadron was soon detached from 2 SAS for operations within Italy, where the German front was crumbling after the collapse of the Gothic Line, and the SAS were needed to stiffen and train Italian partisan units harrassing the Germans' withdrawal across the Alps. To be exact, Farran was forbidden to go along on this operation, but he accompanied his men in the leading aircraft to supervise the drop and managed to 'fall out' over the dropping zone. Here, in the mountains of the Appenines, north of Florence, the SAS were to give training and assistance to a motley group of Italian partisans. Farran's first decision was to radio back to base for a Scots piper, complete with kilt, feeling that the presence of a piper would do a great deal to stiffen the sinews of his rag-tail partisan army. Thus encouraged, they went to war.

The Germans, though retreating, were not cowed. They could and did mount attacks against the partisan forces, and after beating off several attacks on their mountain stronghold, Farran decided to make an all-out attack on the German corps headquarters at Albinea in the valley of the Po which had organised these assaults.

The German headquarters was established in two buildings, separated from the Appenine foothills by a number of small houses, in which the defending troops were billeted. Of the two main buildings, one – the Villa Calvi – was the chief of staff's villa and contained the operations room, while the other – the Villa Rossi – was the residence of the corps commander. Between these two villas ran the main road, and each was permanently guarded by at least four sentries. There were also six machine-gun positions sited round the camp at strategic points, and a closely-meshed defensive perimeter of wire entanglements.

Farran decided to concentrate his attention on the two important villas. Having sited his men close to the target he would place his main force in a semi-circle to the south, thereby isolating the buildings from any support which might come from the garrison. This done, ten British SAS troopers would force entry into each villa, killing the sentries, and they would at once be reinforced by twenty Italian partisans at each building. Then, all hell would be let loose.

After explaining the plan, Farran had to persuade the Italians that by attacking the German headquarters they would have a much greater hope of survival than by just staying where they were in the hills. Nothing could be done without a long discussion, but eventually the partisans accepted Farran's plan and Kirkpatrick, the Scots piper, complete with kilt, then played 'Blue Bonnets Over the Border' as a grand finale to the conference.

From their positions in the mountains they could see through their binoculars that the files of Germans in blue-grey uniforms were marching up into the hills towards the village of Baiso, below the partisan hideout. Farran decided that these troops were going into billets for the night, but at first light the partisans were again on the lookout, gazing towards Baiso. All day there were rumours of further German advances, until the partisans became very jumpy and all threatened to withdraw over the Secchia ridge, deeper into the mountains, and abandon their attack on the German position. Fortunately, most of the rumours proved to be false and when evening came they were still unattacked. Deciding that the order should be given to start, Farran and his group began marching out, along narrow tracks, by passing Baiso to the west. The column trudged along in silence, the leading files lying flat at every track or fence and everyone coming up behind following suit. Then two SAS scouts would creep forward with an advance guard and, when all was found to be clear, they would wave the advance on. Occasionally they would stop for a drink or to question a peasant at some lonely farm as to the whereabouts of the Germans. At every house the dogs barked, and then dogs all over the hills would take it up, so their approach march was nowhere near as quiet as Farran might have wished, but eventually they reached the main road in the floor of the valley, still undetected by enemy patrols.

They had to cross Highway 63, near the village of Casa del Pazzi, which was known to be occupied by a force of *Feldgendarmarie*, the German security police. Unfortunately, just as they were approaching Casa del Pazzi they lost their way. One of the Italian partisans, who said that he knew the area well, claimed that the guide had taken them out of their way. Dark mutterings of treachery filled the air. They passed close to Casa del Pazzi in bright moonlight, as usual disturbing the dogs which began to bark. It seemed certain that they must be seen by the sentries, but nothing happened and they reached the top of a steep hill above the main road.

The going became a little easier as they moved into the lower foothills, and at first light they reached their lying-up position for the day at Casa del Lupo. An SAS scout quickly explored the buildings and found them empty. According to the farmer no Germans had been in the area for the last two days and dawn broke through a thick mist as the main party arrived and took shelter for the day.

Everyone squeezed into the large farmhouse and slept in lofts and ox-sheds, while sentries manned Bren guns at the upstairs windows. A party went off to look at the target and returned around five o'clock reporting that everything seemed normal in Albinea.

The mist was still thick in the evening, providing much useful cover but making navigation difficult. A man from the farm agreed to take them down to the main road, and they wound their way in three columns down the steep hillside, knee-deep now in long, wet grass. Suddenly they were looking out over the valley of the Po at clusters of lights which showed them where the towns were. By now they were within a few miles of their target, and excitement began to grow among the troops.

They reached the main road to Albinea more quickly than anticipated and found it deserted and free of traffic. In small groups the men raced across and wriggled under the hedge on the far side, several dropping into a waterlogged dyke. Once again the noise of their advance seemed far too loud, with the steady barking of the dogs to mark their passage. Yet not a soul stirred in the nearby houses.

Soon the Villa Calvi became visible in the moonlight – a large white house, sitting on a small hill. No lights were showing, and Farran wondered if the Germans were actually there at all. Slightly behind it, to the right, was the Villa Rossi, the corps commander's residence. It was easy to recognise the layout from the air photographs, and everything else soon slotted into place. The SAS could pick out the guardroom and the telephone exchange where they believed two machine-guns were positioned. Further to the right were the troops' billets. The only snag was that everything was so very quiet. Farran felt more than a little alarmed. Had their approach been detected after all?

The attacking force moved on to an assembly position near the Villa Calvi, where Farran sent for his sub-commander and pointed out their target. There, by the telephone exchange, were two Spandau machine-guns. Over there were the troop billets of the garrison; another party would deal with them. Farran wished his men luck and arranged to give them three minutes to get in position, and then with his ten British SAS soldiers, moved off quickly to the attack.

Just as the British had started to climb the hill, they noticed that they were crossing a minefield. The Italians followed them, albeit a little reluctantly. Then, just as they cleared the minefield, a long burst of fire was heard from the Villa Calvi and red, white and green tracer bullets flew in every direction. A hundred men had infiltrated the position unobserved, but the Germans were by no means asleep and, as always, quick to react. Spandaus began quickly spraying the area from the south. Farran thought that some of his men were firing in the wrong direction, but soon realised that there were not two, but at least seven, German machine-guns in action around the defensive perimeter. Piper Kirkpatrick was ordered to strike up 'Highland Laddie' to let the Germans know that they had British troops to deal with, but Kirkpatrick had only played a couple of bars when a searching Spandau found his position. Kirkpatrick slid swiftly into a ditch but carried on playing.

Meanwhile, an SAS soldier, Ken Harvey, had killed two sentries on the lawns of Villa Calvi and blown in the front door of the villa with a rocket from a bazooka. Four more Germans were killed on the ground floor as the SAS and their allies burst in, but other Germans fought back on the spiral staircase. Throwing open the door of one room, Harvey was met by a big German soldier armed with a Schmeisser. Harvey ducked and his sergeant, following behind, cut the German down with a burst from his tommy-gun. The Germans kept up a heavy fire from the first floor and made it impossible for the British to ascend the stairs. One man was wounded by a grenade which came rolling down from above and another SAS man was hit in the legs by a burst of Schmeisser fire.

By now close-quarter fighting was raging all around the position and a furious cross-fire was taking place between the lawn outside the villa and the Germans firing from the top windows. Several Germans were killed by tommy-gun fire and bazooka rockets but Ken Harvey realised that it would be impossible to take the house in the twenty minutes Farran had decreed. He decided to burn the place down. Working desperately against time, the SAS piled up everything burnable – chairs, curtains, paper from files and maps – into a great heap in the middle of the operations room. To this they added a few pounds of explosive, sprinkled a bottle of petrol about and threw in a match. Soon the whole house was ablaze.

Over at the corps commander's house, operations had not been so successful. When Harvey had opened fire at Calvi, a siren on the roof of Villa Rossi began to wail and all the outside lights went on. The SAS patrol commander killed four sentries with his tommy-gun and then made a dash for the open door of the villa, but a hail of bullets met him at the foot of the staircase. Someone shot out the lights and four more Germans were killed and two surrendered, but although several attempts were made to climb the stairs, all were unsuccessful. In these assaults one SAS sergeant was shot in the head and another SAS man was seriously wounded as he tried to rally the attackers on the first landing. Then the patrol commander was killed on the ground floor. The Germans attempted to rush down the stairs but gave up when three of their number were killed on the upper landing by grenades, one of them the commanding general. As a group of soldiers started a fire in the kitchen, the wounded were moved outside onto the lawns.

The battle was now reaching its height with bullets flying all over the place and, above the gunfire, the sound of Kirkpatrick's pipes. The Italians were returning the German fire, firing star-shells to illuminate the scene, but Farran was aware that their ammunition must be almost exhausted. The Villa Calvi was now well ablaze, and the Villa Rossi was beginning to burn. Enough was enough – Farran raised his Very pistol and fired a red light into the sky as the signal to withdraw.

As always in such SAS operations, getting away was the hard part. They moved away in small groups, heading due west to the river Crostollo, the various parties gathering together on the far side of the river. Farran found himself with almost all the British SAS, a few partisans and two wounded men. They headed towards temporary safety on the south side of the main road. Two men, Private Burke and Ramos, a Spaniard, refused to leave the badly wounded Mike Lees, and they carried his fifteen-stone frame for four days across the plains, now swarming with angry Germans, until they reached a safe hiding place in the hills where he could be looked after. Farran later arranged for Lees to be picked up from a makeshift landing ground in the foothills and flown back to Florence. For their bravery, Ramos and Burke were later awarded the Military Medal. A number of Italian wounded were also evacuated. The total casualties had been three killed and six taken prisoner.

The retreating force marched west as fast as they could, the sky behind them lit by the flames from the villas. German transport was now moving along the main road to the south, as the raiders assembled on the bank of the Crostollo and struck south towards the road. A mistake in navigation almost led them into an anti-aircraft battery but fortunately the German signpost was sighted just in time. At last they were able to cross the main road, and found a farm where they were able to leave one of the wounded, having made arrangements for him to be smuggled up the mountains when fit enough to travel.

Back at their rendezvous at Casa del Lupo, a horse was requisitioned for another wounded man, for the whole countryside was now alive with German troops and it was impossible to halt. Fortunately the mist was still thick, but rain had made the narrow mountain paths treacherous. Still, everyone was delighted by the raid and after marching non-stop for 22 hours, they crossed the Secchia undetected by the wide-ranging German patrols. They passed through the partisan lines near Carpenti without incident and marched home in formation through the village of Vallestra, behind Kirkpatrick's pipes.

Farran's SAS group in Italy had a difficult task, politically as well as militarily. Many of the partisan groups, well armed, and with such glamorous names as The Green Flames, or The Grey Wolves, were none too keen to attack the common enemy. They were more interested in acquiring arms and prestige ready for a post-war struggle for control of Italy, and many groups owed direct allegiance to Moscow and were hoping for the arrival of the Red Army now fighting across Yugoslavia to the east. Farran and his men had to tread gently and avoid politics, while urging their confederates to get on with the war.

The main task of the SAS and the partisan allies was to slow down and disrupt the German withdrawal from Italy, particularly as the Germans tried to transfer fighting units to Germany where the Allied advance was now sweeping up to the Rhine. To do this the SAS had to attack continually and in so doing the SAS were highly successful. Ever adaptable, the SAS also discovered the use of heavy mortars and field artillery against German transport and soon brought these weapons into play behind the lines.

SAS Corporal Larley commanded a 37-millimetre cannon positioned in the hills by Ligonchio. Larley fired his last twenty rounds directly into the German garrison positions at Busana on Highway 63 before he left and when asked why he had used up all the 37-mil ammunition he replied that he had to do something after having had Busana fully in his sights for a fortnight. The Germans, considerably shaken, promptly withdrew as well. On another occasion, Farran used a 75-millimetre howitzer to attack the main German route to the north, Highway 12, at Sassuolo, which was full of transport. 'When we had bracketed the target,' he writes, 'we fired five rounds rapid, which sounded like a stick of bombs as they burst on the ground. Occasionally though the only response to my order to fire was a clanging sound as the crew endeavoured to free a jammed case with a crowbar. Many shells had been damaged in their parachute descent, and their cases were so distorted that they jammed in the breech.' Seventy shells were fired in total, and hits were seen on the anti-aircraft battery protecting Sassuolo, on the Hotel Italia which was the German headquarters, and on a factory occupied by the Germans. As soon as the shells had been fired, Farran and his men hitched up the howitzer behind a jeep and set off to repeat the process somewhere else before the enemy could reply.

They learned shortly afterwards that early the following day a full battalion of German troops occupied their gun position overlooking Sassuolo and stayed there until the British army broke through.

The artillery technique seemed so effective and so

simple to carry out that on 17 April Farran sent Lieutenant Eld with a three-inch mortar detachment to attack other targets in the area. Thirty mortar bombs smashed into Boglioni where 250 enemy troops were garrisoned. The enemy headquarters was hit and only a few rifle-shots were fired in Eld's direction. The enemy evacuated the village the same night.

Meanwhile, the Italian partisan bands were also in action. Two nights after Eld attacked Boglioni the Italians carried out a highly successful ambush on Highway 12. Two small parties, under British NCOs, penetrated a heavily populated German area near Selva. Corporal Ford's party of five men attacked a column of ten armoured half-tracks, escorting fifteen trucks. They set five trucks on fire – an action for which Ford was later awarded the Military Medal.

The next night more Italians, under Eyton-Jones, attacked Montebonello, a village on Highway 12 which held a large number of Germans. The Italians harrassed the garrison with sniping and machine-gun fire and the enemy return fire went on until well into the following morning, some considerable time after the raiders had actually left.

While these attacks were tormenting the Germans north of the Po, the American Fifth Army had broken through near Bologna and the whole German army was flung into full retreat. Reconnaissance revealed that all roads were crammed nose to tail with German transport, and tempting targets were available to the SAS.

Farran split his forces to attack in as many places as possible, detaching a section under Eld with orders to mortar Scandiano, the nearest town of any importance on the Lombardy plain. The rest of the force moved up to the foothills overlooking the Po Valley, occupying a main position on a hill, commanding the crossings over the river Secchia. One of these was the bridge at Sassuolo and the other a ford. Farran sited two Vickers medium machine-guns on the forward slope of the hill and placed a high angle 75-millimetre howitzer immediately behind the hill, using an old slit-trench on the forward slope as an observation point. From here Farran could watch the continuous stream of trucks, gun carriages and ammunition lorries making their way across the river. To the east a similar stream of vehicles was crossing the Sassuolo bridge, making their way along the foot of the hills scarcely 500 yards away from Farran's position.

The target was tempting and the SAS remained undetected, but there was a snag. A German infantry battalion was resting under the trees at the foot of the hill just below. Farran watched them through his fieldglasses and pondered, for if he opened fire they would probably counter-attack up the hill, and Farran's men did not have enough fire power to resist them. Farran was unwilling to plunge his men into a pitched battle, preferring, as was SAS policy, to attack only when complete surprise was on their side. Eventually, the sight of all that transport proved too tempting. Farran took up the radio and spoke to the howitzer position.

'Right! Fifteen hundred yards, one round – HE – fire!'

A shell whistled high overhead and exploded on the far side of the river, north of the enemy columns.

'Down one hundred. HE – fire!'

After three ranging shots a lorry towing a gun was hit and capsized in the middle of the ford, causing an almighty traffic jam and much confusion.

Then the Vickers was ordered to fire on any target they saw on the road in front, and soon thick columns of smoke were rising up from lorries which had been set on fire. Meanwhile, the German infantry remained in the trees and only occasional single shots could be heard. Farran was uncertain whether this was the enemy firing back or the Italian partisans giving their support to the Vickers. Howitzer shells were still crashing around the ford and the enemy was in a state of total confusion. Twelve trucks were now on fire in the river, and more were burning along the road; horses bolted, carts overturned and then a flight of Spitfires drawn by the smoke and seeing the columns in the ford dived down to add their weight to the attack, strafing in long sweeps along the road and river.

The howitzer and Vickers were now turned on the Sassuolo bridge. Within minutes three well-aimed shells had destroyed five enemy lorries and another jam blocked the road. The battle raged all day, with very little retaliation from the enemy infantry, and towards the evening, having fired over 150 shells, Farran hitched up his artillery and withdrew his force into the hills, all well contented with a good day's work.

The SAS continued to harrass the German army all the way back across the Alpine passes, pressing home their attacks against declining opposition, destroying a great deal of equipment and demoralising many formations which might otherwise have got back safely to Germany, ready to fight again. These attacks also helped the main Allied armies fighting their way north in Italy.

Not only did the small scattered SAS teams carry out many of these attacks, they also organised and encouraged the Italian partisan bands to come out of the hills and fight on the plains, eventually driving the enemy, stubborn fighters though they were, from their last toehold in Italy.

6

JEEP WARFARE IN FRANCE
1944

The SAS role in the 1944 battle for Normandy was another task which went beyond those well-tried guidelines for SAS operations laid down by David Stirling and practised with such success by his immediate followers and successors. Their assignment was to prevent German reinforcements reaching the Normandy battlefield from Germany and Southern France and as in Italy, to cooperate closely with the Resistance fighters, the Maquis. The Maquis put around 100,000 guerrilla fighters, men and women, into the field on D-Day with the aim of disrupting German supply routes and the flow of reinforcements to the front, while the Allied armies established a firm beachhead and built up their forces for the breakout. This Maquis activity needed constant support and re-supply, which the Allied planners hoped to provide by continual parachute drops of men and arms and the infiltration of SAS squadrons on the ground. The SAS mobility and firepower would, it was felt, greatly increase the operational effectiveness of the locally based and lightly equipped French Maquis fighters.

This supporting role so restricted the normally free-wheeling SAS techniques for striking at targets of opportunity, that Lt-Col Bill Stirling of 2 SAS felt unable to accept the task and resigned his command, which was then given to Lt-Col Brian Franks. Eventually, under continued SAS pressure, the planners redrafted the SAS operational orders to allow them more scope for action on the ground, and some 2000 SAS soldiers, fully armed and equipped with jeeps, were dropped or infiltrated behind the enemy lines in France in the weeks before or just after D-Day, 6 June 1944. Once behind the German lines, they established firm forest bases, built up their strength by parachute drops, and proceeded to harrass the enemy. One good example of SAS operations is Roy Farran's activities along the Loire.

Roy Farran's squadron, from 2 SAS, went to France with twenty jeeps in August, landing on a recently captured airfield near Rennes in Brittany. Within the day they were weaving their way through the enemy lines to the country of the river Loire, settling in a forest close to the town of Orleans, heading for the big SAS base, in the Forêt de Châtillon.

They drove down deserted forest rides through the trees and onto the main road at the village of Les Bordes on the banks of the Loire. The streets of the village were full of Maquis fighters, from whom they learned that there were large German columns in three nearby villages, Gien, Montargis and Sully. Farran was loaned a guide and before moving east he sent a jeep patrol to check out the Montargis road. The patrol returned, reporting that the village was clear, but the SAS decided to move along minor roads and country lanes where they would be reasonably safe.

This infiltration across heavily occupied country was tricky work, for the Germans were everywhere, and were thoroughly alert. When Farran's party had to cross a main road, a patrol was sent forward to report if the road was clear of enemy armour. If all was well, the jeeps would drive across at top speed in column. However, in crossing the main Montargis road, the first jeep became separated from the rest and instead of rejoining the end of the column when the others were safely across, stayed on guard there until dawn the next day. Having lost contact with the remainder of the squadron, the commander, Sergeant Forster, led his jeep alone across France and eventually rejoined the squadron in the Forêt de Châtillon. Among many incidents along the way, he collided with a German staff car at a road junction and shot the four high-ranking enemy officers riding inside.

Meanwhile, Farran's force was drifting south and east towards Burgundy, gathering information on the way, getting used to the feel of this closely wooded country with its friendly population and ever-threatening German columns.

Farran was reluctant to start active operations until they had reached the SAS base at Châtillon, but his force was making good time and he decided to finish the journey quickly by night. In the event this proved an unwise move, since the complete air cover provided by Allied aircraft during the day had forced the Germans to move under cover of darkness. In fact, the best time for the British infiltrators to move was around midday. For the night move, Farran divided his squadron into three sections – five jeeps under Ramon, eight under himself, and the remainder under Lt David Leigh, who had led SAS jeep patrols in the desert campaign.

Farran's party eventually arrived at the village of Mailly-le-Château in Burgundy, where an extremely agitated Frenchman jumped on the jeep, yelling that the enemy were in the village and he would lead the SAS troops into battle. Farran had to silence him at pistol point, and it was a long time before he could get any information from the other villagers, but it appeared that the Germans were on the other side of the river and Ramon's party had passed through, shooting their way out of trouble but losing a jeep to machine-gun fire. The Frenchman, now much calmer, led the SAS jeeps down the hill to the river, where Farran went ahead on foot. Walking around a corner, he was met with a raking burst of Spandau fire. Farran flung himself into the ditch and saw about a hundred German infantry with horse-drawn vehicles under the trees. Farran's men fired a few bursts of tracer at them from the top of a cliff above the river and managed to set a cart on fire before withdrawing to the village and moving off again to the south.

That night they caught up with Ramon and his party in the Forêt de St Jean near Avallon, more than 100 miles behind the enemy lines. On the following day Ramon, with two jeeps, went ahead once again but just outside the forest he met with more trouble. In the village of Villaines, near Semur, he ran into a number of ex-Afrika Korps troops and both his jeeps were destroyed by their prompt attack and accurate fire. Ramon managed to escape on foot into the hills, but three men with him were captured, and no warning was passed to Farran's column following close behind.

Unaware of the ambush ahead, Farran was travelling at the head of his column, when he came face to face with a 75-millimetre gun aimed point blank down the road. Abandoning their jeep the crew hurled themselves into a ditch as two Germans in Afrika Korps hats opened fire at close range. The jeep was wrecked, bursting into flames, while machine-gun bullets laced the road and hedges.

German soldiers were spraying the jeeps with machine-gun fire as the SAS swung them about and commenced to fire back. Farran's party, now on foot, still had a Bren and managed to hold the enemy off from a gully while the others withdrew. Farran then broke away and doubled back down the road to stop any oncoming jeeps, and finding a convenient point down the lane, two of the jeeps fired at close range into the German's flank as they left the ambush and began to sweep in on the trapped SAS men. Corporal Clarke was still holding out with the Bren, and Sergeant-Major Mitchell with ten men and four Brens held the line of the hedge, while Farran commanded two jeeps in the middle of the road. The fire-fight raged about this position and the enemy fire became very heavy, with field artillery and mortar now in action. But then the German infantry unwisely charged in along both sides of the road, giving the SAS a magnificent field of fire. German casualties were heavy, but instead of retreating the Germans pressed on until they had penetrated the SAS positions and were being fired on from all three sides.

This little battle raged on for almost an hour until, under cover of the guns, Farran and his men were able to withdraw. They made their way across country to emerge near Joux, where they learned that an entire Panzer division was now deployed across their path in the villages between Semur and Montbard. Getting to their rendezvous was proving difficult.

The much depleted SAS force drove on throughout the night, making a wide detour to the south after losing their way in the numerous lanes and cart tracks well off the main roads. In the morning, out of the original twenty jeeps, they could count only seven. Casualties to date included the desert veteran David Leigh, killed by the German column at Villaines. But Farran was determined to keep going until they reached shelter at Châtillon. They had to drive very slowly along the summer-dry tracks, for otherwise the dust cloud behind them would soon have given their whereabouts away to enemy patrols.

On the morning after the fight, they halted by a closed level-crossing where, before they had time to take cover, a train came into view. As it drew near they saw it was a goods train with about twenty trucks, and as the engine drew level with the crossing gates ahead, Farran gave his men the order to fire. Vickers 'K' guns poured in tracers and armour-piercing bullets at close range, and rifles and Brens soon joined in. The train chugged slowly on for a couple of hundred yards, the boiler shrouded in bursts of steam, until it rolled to a stop with steam escaping from all over the engine. The Germans in the rear carriages were all killed, but the French engine driver jumped from his train and joined the SAS to watch the flames devour the carriages.

Later that morning they had almost reached their objective in the southern boundary of the Forêt de Châtillon when Jim Mackie noticed a German radar post among the trees. While the SAS column was studying this, a number of machine-guns opened fire on them, but since it was difficult to see where this fire was coming from, they felt it would be better to withdraw, at least for the moment. Later that day the Germans evacuating this position were attacked by the SAS and sustained 35 casualties, and that afternoon Farran's battered jeeps rolled at last into the main SAS base, where dozens of SAS and Maquis were ready to attack the enemy.

The SAS already at Châtillon had by now carried out several attacks, and these increased after Farran's arrival. On 28 August they knocked out five trucks on roads around the forest and laid mines on the Langres-Dijon road. Later that day they obtained information that there was a German operations headquarters in a farm near Châtillon, which was considered a good target for the SAS's three-inch mortars. Grant Hibbert and Farran decided to recce this farm, and, if all seemed well, attack it in force the following day.

During this reconnaissance they learned that the farm headquarters was no longer occupied, but that the garrison of Châtillon itself was being relieved by Panzer grenadier infantry from nearby Montbard. There were at present only 150 Germans with twenty trucks within the town, although more were expected, so the two SAS officers decided to attack without delay.

Making their way back to base along the Dijon road, Hibbert and Farran were turning off into the forest when they saw a convoy of four German trucks coming towards Châtillon along a parallel road. Thinking these might contain the expected reinforcements they turned their jeep around and drove back rapidly, hoping to engage the trucks at the junction, but a Maquis ambush fired on the enemy first. When Farran and Hibbert drove up the Frenchmen were firing down from the side of the hills, while the Germans were retaliating from the ditches along the road. Then the Vickers 'K's opened up at close range from behind the enemy and many German soldiers were killed. In the brief fire-fight, three of the trucks were destroyed.

The combined forces of the Maquis and the SAS squadron then attacked Châtillon at dawn. Farran's plan was to first occupy the important junction of the Montbard and Dijon roads and from there send a party equipped with Brens to attack the German position in the town château from the north. The explosion of a three-inch mortar bomb on that château would be the signal for the main attack to commence.

Jim Mackie reached and occupied the crossroads position unhindered and Farran moved out in nine jeeps with 40 men to the town centre. They occupied all the main roads leading to the market square and two jeeps were detached to block the Troyes-Chaumont crossroads. Finally all the telephone wires were cut and with the unsuspecting German garrison now isolated, the attack began.

First the SAS mortared the château, hitting the target with 48 bombs. Fifteen minutes after the firing started a column of about 30 German trucks, two loaded with ammunition, burst into flames and exploded and the battle then raged fiercely, with Bren guns and Vickers engaging Spandau and Schmeisser to the steady crash of the three-inch mortars. Soon the Germans had their mortars in action and small-arms fire could be heard from the centre of the town as well as from the rear of the château, although the main battle was taking place around Mackie's position at the Montbard-Dijon crossroads.

Around eleven o'clock, word came to Farran that a number of Germans were fighting their way down the main street from the château, and that everything was so chaotic in the town centre that the Germans were actually mortaring their own side. Even so, Mackie was under strong pressure: the Montbard relief column was becoming more organised and their fire more accurate. The promised Maquis reinforcements had still not arrived, so Farran decided to break off the attack. Hibbert met up with 60 of the promised 500 Maquis, whom he led into the town, sending a message to Farran to join him in a second attack on the château. Farran first posted jeep ambushes on all the main roads leading into the town, which soon destroyed eight German vehicles packed with troops. Then, with Jim Mackie giving covering fire from a jeep, Farran led a foot patrol round to the east of Châtillon, where they were surprised to come upon German machine-gun posts on each side of a narrow lane.

The Germans manning the first post had their backs to Farran's party, who had decided to assault the position on the left when their presence in the lane was discovered. Suddenly the whole lane was alive with bullets. High-banked, narrow and straight, the lane was a death-trap for the SAS and bullets whistled past their heads as they sprinted for cover in a farmhouse, running right through the house and out down towards a canal bank, over lock gates, then across country to the east. Two machine-guns fired at them as they ran across the open fields and crawled under cover of a hedge. Here Mackie's jeep arrived to help them. Exhausted, they finally reached a friendly farm and managed to return to base. The day-long battle for Châtillon ended with 100 Germans dead and many more wounded, and at least ten trucks destroyed. SAS and Maquis casualties were slight.

On the following day, Farran took the squadron to another base further south near Auberive. Here they received a supply drop of seven more jeeps. These brought their total vehicle strength to eighteen, which Hibbert and Farran reorganised into three patrols. Each took enough men to operate nine jeeps, and left the remaining troopers to operate on foot in the Chaumont area. The plan was for two patrols to advance on parallel roads east towards the Belfort Gap, where the Germans were said to be re-grouping, having retreated in front of the Third and Seventh US Armies. From a position near Belfort, Farran and Hibbert hoped to join other SAS forces operating in the province of Alsace-Lorraine. Farran planned to get there by advancing through the Forêt de Darney, while Grant planned to travel through the area north of Bourbonne, where he soon came across a large petrol dump and a number of trucks, which he promptly attacked and destroyed.

While rolling east on the minor roads and tracks, the SAS carried out successful ambushes on the main highways, and once established at the new SAS base, operations began again against transport columns and enemy headquarters. However, the SAS did not have it all their own way. Enemy patrols soon located the SAS positions and summoned up forces for a counter-attack.

One evening in early September 1944, a Maquis scout from a nearby village rushed into the SAS headquarters to warn them that 600 German infantry supported by four armoured cars with troop-carriers and a staff car had arrived from Granrupt. The SAS position was enclosed by woodland and the only way out for the jeeps was via a lane leading directly towards the Germans in Granrupt. Small-arms fire had already broken out on the eastern edge of the woodlands near the resupply drop zone, which was all too clearly marked by white parachutes from a recent drop still caught in the higher branches of the trees. The Maquis in the forest were in a state of confusion and escape to the east and the north was impossible. Farran could find no way out, for a deep stream ran through the woods to the northern edge and the jeeps would be unable to cross this. With the German cordon closing in, a small gap was found in the south-west corner of the wood, through which the jeeps crashed into open country. Here they found a good track and made their way out to the main road, from where, their retreat secure, Farran sent Lieutenant Gurney with two jeeps to attack the enemy's rear. A group of German infantry was successfully machine-gunned and an SAS ambush on the road near Nennezel set fire to two staff cars, killing the colonel and second-in-command of the German force.

During that night Farran's men laid mines on the roads around Darney, a very effective way of hitting at the enemy, and as soon as the mining patrols returned, the SAS moved on across the river Saône to the south-east, heading out of trouble. The enemy was still active on the ground as the SAS drew closer to the main junction of two lines of retreat being taken by German forces from the north and west, so at each main road mines were laid. Around Luxeuil-les-Bains in the Jura, the enemy seemed to be even more numerous and, inevitably, the presence of Farran's party was soon discovered. There was very little cover available in the way of deep forest, but they managed to hide up for a while in an area of small copses about two miles square. From here Farran led his jeep column out onto a main track through the trees and turned to the south, but the three leading jeeps were soon stuck in soft mud and unable to move. The jeeps were hurriedly camouflaged with branches while the men took cover, listening carefully as the pursuing German patrols came crashing all about them through the trees.

These German patrols failed to locate them and withdrew at dusk. That night it rained heavily again, but in the morning they were at last able to dig the jeeps out and manhandle them back down the track, not daring to give away their position by starting up the engines. After hours of toil they finally managed to get out of the woods and head towards a thicker forest to the north of Luxeuil-les-Bains, where they met a small group of Maquis fighters, who provided them with guides and helped them set up another base.

From this base the SAS carried out several successful operations, although they also suffered casualties. Hugh Gurney took on one German column at close range in the village of Velorcey. His first bullets hit a truck loaded with ammunition and men on both sides were blown to bits in the subsequent explosion. Gurney escaped from his wrecked jeep but was shot down in the road by a Spandau. Another new SAS officer, Lieutenant Burtwhistle, led a raid on a German horse-drawn column in Fontaines-les-Bains, shot up a number of Germans and fired several carts, but on the way back one of his jeeps was blown up and three men were wounded.

The numbers and strength of Germans on the roads forced Farran's party further into the woods to a new position. Here the jeeps were carefully camouflaged, for German infantry had dug themselves in near the edge of the forest, while a battery of 88-millimetre guns became established only 100 yards away; the lurking SAS could even hear the German gunners talking to each other. A couple of foot patrols went out to try to contact the advancing Americans but were soon forced to return because of the number of German patrols in the area. They did, however, manage to succeed in mining many of the roads and the railways still being used by the Germans.

American artillery eventually began counter-battery fire against the nearby German guns, and although many of the shells landed around the British hiding in the woods, there were no casualties among them. Two days later the Germans withdrew and on the following morning an American armoured car patrol, guided by the Maquis, arrived at the position and Operation Wallace was over. Farran's men took their time re-crossing France, passing the scenes of their recent exploits during their month behind enemy lines. Hibbert's patrol rejoined Farran's at Arromanches on the Normandy coast and the squadron returned together to Southampton.

7

'OPERATION HOUNDSWORTH'
1944–5

Although Farran's operation covered the largest distance behind the enemy lines, it was just one of about 40 such SAS operations which sapped German strength in the months after D-Day. The total SAS score in 1944 is remarkable: 7500 enemy soldiers killed or wounded; 4700 taken prisoner; 7600 vehicles of various types destroyed; 29 railway engines blown up; 164 railway lines wrecked. It adds up to a steady, relentless pressure on enemy positions, manpower and vital supply lines.

1 SAS's 'Operation Houndsworth' which, like Farran's took place in Burgundy and Eastern France, began on 7 June, just after D-Day. At one time the squadrons of 1 SAS effectively controlled hundreds of miles of enemy territory south of Dijon from bases in the deep woods of the Morvan forest, ideal country for guerrilla warfare, from which the enemy were subjected to constant SAS attacks.

'Houndsworth' itself was the name for an operational base established in the thickly wooded mountainous slopes of the Morvan. In August Lieutenant Harrison arrived with a full SAS squadron in some two dozen jeeps, aiming to relieve an SAS force due to go home. Also at 'Houndsworth' at this time was Lieutenant Alec Muirhead, who had a reputation for laying highly successful ambushes. Alec Muirhead took his mortar section down into the town of Autun, where the Germans were operating a synthetic petrol plant. Having kept their position under observation during the day, Muirhead knew it to be well guarded with strong infantry and even anti-aircraft guns, making it extremely difficult to get men into the plant. At 01.30 that night, therefore, in clear moonlight, the SAS party took up their positions outside the plant, setting up their mortars within easy range. When all was ready, Muirhead gave the order to open rapid fire. The mortar bombs' high explosive and phosphorous hit their target with a satisfactory series of crashes and flashes of flame. Bomb after bomb went crashing into the plant, a rapid total of 40 high explosive and incendiary projectiles, which soon had the petrol plant ablaze. The plant was still burning three days later. This 1 SAS squadron carried out a number of successful operations over an area of approximately 6000 square miles: mining, ambushing, derailing trains, blowing bridges, cutting a wide swathe of destruction at little cost to themselves.

The 'Houndsworth' SAS squadrons usually received excellent co-operation from the Maquis headquarters at nearby Chalaux, and although it was definitely not SAS policy to work too closely with the Maquis, there were many times when events brought them together. Out on one patrol, SAS Sergeant Du Vivier heard an enormous explosion from the area of Entrains, where the Maquis had blown up the railway line, hoping to delay the departure of a munitions train for the front. Du Vivier sent a message to the workmen who were repairing the line asking them to hold up the repairs long enough for his three-man patrol to move up the line toward Cosne, the train's next destination.

Each carrying 30 lb of explosives, the three SAS men, travelling on borrowed bicycles, went unchallenged by the Germans, even though they rode through two towns wearing British battledress. The whole operation of laying the charges took two hours as they had to dig away with their bare hands, working quietly so as not to alert any German patrol with the slightest noise. Having completed their mission, they returned their cycles to the Maquis and went back to Houndsworth. When their charges went off, two railway engines were completely wrecked together with a wagon crammed with ammunition; ten other wagons were derailed.

Shortly afterwards the SAS at Houndsworth learned that the Germans were about to attack the Maquis headquarters at Chalaux. An SAS officer, Bill Fraser, contacted the Maquis and together they drew up a joint plan for the defence of this position. Their main element was the possession of a 6 lb field gun, parachuted in to the SAS, and this they positioned on a forward slope commanding a good view of all the roads leading into Chalaux. A Bren gun team then dug in to support the gun crew, and the other SAS soldiers and Maquis fighters took up ambush positions on the roads and in the woods. Early the next morning they saw a German column coming along the main road towards Chalaux and this was engaged by the Maquis. As soon as the Maquis posts went into action the main German body halted, but a forward group continued on past the first ambush, coming under fire from a second Maquis position, while the first Maquis group continued to engage the main body. Then the SAS Bren gun on the hill went into action to support the French, but the six-pounder remained silent, waiting for a worthwhile target.

As the firing rose in volume and the battle developed, two German staff cars were seen speeding along the road towards Chalaux. The six-pounder fired a round at them at 1000 yards range and missed, but this sudden burst of artillery caused the German cars to withdraw rapidly, the officers sending forward a German machine-gun with fifteen infantrymen in support. The six-pounder put it out of action with three rounds and the infantry scattered to take cover behind a stone wall. Five shells spaced at five-yard intervals destroyed this protection and a further two rounds of shell-fire wrecked a second machine-gun post, after which the Germans began to retreat for another think.

All was fairly quiet until late in the afternoon, when two German mortars took up positions behind a small hill, out of range of the field-gun, and the Germans positioned a machine-gun out in the open, hoping to draw the six-pounder's fire so that their quite accurate 81-millimetre mortars could knock it out. This trick didn't work; the SAS Bren team moved down the hill to engage the enemy Spandau and the Germans were again forced to withdraw.

The next German infantry attack met with more success. The first Maquis position by the road was overrun and the SAS field gun team found themselves outflanked. They removed the breech-piece from the gun and camouflaged it before withdrawing into the Maquis lines. In the evening the Germans halted the attack and withdrew. The Maquis and SAS had held off an all-out attack for a full day, killed a number of the enemy and escaped without loss.

The SAS in France contained its fair share of characters, and many of these were private soldiers. Trooper Jemson was one of a small party under Captain Wellstead which set out from 'Houndsworth' during July to blow up the main railway line between Digoin and Paray-le Monial. The SAS party reached the line just after midnight and began to lay the charges. Captain Wellstead left Jemson with his Bren gun to guard their line of retreat over a double bridge across the nearby river and canal. Jemson took up his position in a ditch between the two bridges on the west of the road. He had been ordered not to fire if a German patrol should come into view unless the Germans fired first.

Jemson heard the sound of a platoon of Germans approaching quietly down each side of the canal and coming closer along the riverbank while the sabotage party was still digging holes to lay their charges. The Germans soon heard the sounds coming from the railway and took up positions astride both bridges, probably hoping to ambush the SAS on their way out. A Spandau was brought and positioned in a ditch directly across from where Jemson lay, exactly four yards away, wondering what to do.

Not daring to move a muscle, Jemson lay perfectly still, stuck between the Germans and the noise of the SAS on the railway line above. Finally, the sounds of digging from the railway track stopped and the SAS party began to withdraw towards their rendezvous. As they reached the first bridge the German Spandau opened fire, but at the same time Jemson opened up point-blank with his Bren, killing the machine-gun crew instantly. Jemson then hurled himself from cover and rolled down the bank toward the low ground between the river and the canal, from where he fired on the other German ambush positions so accurately that the SAS party managed to return to the railway and set off their charges before escaping into the dark. For well over an hour Jemson battled on alone, dashing from one position to another to cause confusion among the Germans. The fact that they were under fire from just one man didn't seem to dawn on them. When Jemson ran out of Bren ammunition he took on the enemy with his Colt automatic. After the main party had had time to get clear, he dismantled the Bren and threw the parts away, fired the last few rounds from his Colt, dived into the river and escaped

A great deal of the work of the SAS was, and still is, surveillance and intelligence gathering. Frequently a routine patrol would pay off by first detecting a target, assessing the enemy strength and then calling up more firepower for an attack. This was the case when one of the 'Houndsworth' parties detected what was obviously a defensive position. However, they could not immediately discover exactly what was being defended. Moving with their usual caution they infiltrated the outer ring, only to find still heavier inner defences, which clearly indicated a target of vital importance – in fact, Rommel's headquarters.

Such a target was beyond their strength, but the radio was still available and an emergency message was sent to London. A bomber force was promptly despatched to the area. Rommel's headquarters were destroyed, but the field marshal was away when the attack took place and he escaped, only to fall victim to an attack by RAF fighters a few days later.

The Germans went to great lengths to conceal movement of their troops and supply columns and so avoid air attack, but found hiding such activity from the SAS parties on the ground much more difficult. Lieutenant John Tonkin, operating in the Poitiers area, blew up the railway lines around the city several times until it became more and more difficult for the Germans to keep up with the work of constant repair. Arriving one night for another attack, Tonkin and his party ran directly into a German sentry. Hiding until he had safely passed, they moved forward cautiously and found that the Germans had built a spur line from the main railway into the cover of a wood in which the SAS counted eleven railway tankers containing petrol. Here again, their radio was the key. A message was flashed to London and towards dawn Tonkin's men saw RAF rocket-firing Typhoons diving out of the skies above the woods. Within minutes the trees were flaming and the SAS gleefully withdrew.

The SAS regiments – British, French and Belgian – were in action throughout the campaigns in north-west Europe, and Italy, right up to the last days of the war. Operations as described here, small parties or squadrons, chipped away relentlessly at the enemy, and continued fighting until their jeeps rolled to a stop inside the crumbling frontiers of the Reich.

The SAS had done well in four years of war. When World War II broke out they did not exist, and now there was a full brigade of British troops and SAS regiments in the armies of France and Belgium. The Belgian SAS – now the Belgian Para-Commando Regiment – still wears the winged dagger badge and maintains the SAS 'Who Dares, Wins' motto, the only regiment which can trace its history back in an unbroken line to the wartime SAS.

Most of the irregular forces of World War II were broken up or disbanded as soon as the war was over. The Parachute Regiment and the Royal Marine Commandos survived, but many of the rest – the LRDG, Popski's Private Army and the SAS Regiments – were soon disbanded. For a time it seemed as if the SAS concept had died out in the British Army.

8

THE MALAYA SCOUTS
1950–3

The wartime British SAS Regiments were disbanded in October 1945, although the French and Belgian SAS Regiments went on to become component parts of their newly reformed national armies. The future role of an SAS-style regiment was discussed during various post-World War II examinations of the late conflict and a clear need was envisaged for such a formation during any future large-scale war. This led in 1947 to the formation of a Territorial Army SAS unit, the 21 SAS (Artists) TA, which was commanded initially by Lt-Col Brian Franks, the wartime commander of 2 SAS.

Meanwhile, having just emerged from a world war, the British army was beginning its forty years of colonial campaigns in Palestine, where the British mandate ended in 1947, and was followed within days by the first Arab–Israeli war. Then followed a long series of conflicts, long and short, large and small in Malaya, Cyprus, Aden, Borneo, Kenya, the Gulf, as well as in the first and so far only major clash between a Communist power and the Western democracies, the Korean War of 1949–52. And of course, until recently, there was the long drawn out agony of Northern Ireland, which began in 1968.

The typical pattern for these end-of-Empire conflicts was, first, the creation of a liberation movement in the colony and civil disturbance, followed by the imprisonment of the national leaders by the British Government. Then came a sporadic guerrilla war with shootings, ambushes and bombings, followed after some years by the release of the national leaders and a British withdrawal. This was followed, after a short interval, by more conflict, partition and dictatorship. The British army, as usual, got the short end of the stick.

These colonial campaigns eventually provided good scope for SAS-style operations, but in a reversal of their wartime role. Now it was the enemy, the 'patriots', 'guerillas', 'freedom-fighters' or 'terrorists' (the descriptive name depending on whose side the speaker was on) hiding in the countryside or deep in the larger towns who emerged to strike at British troops and targets, while the SAS took on the role of counter-terrorism, pursuing the terrorists into the deepest jungle, or the most remote mountain lair. This was to be the pattern of post-war SAS activity – a role that began in 1950 during the Malaya Emergency.

During World War II, resistance to the Japanese in Malaya had been largely Communist-inspired, aided, certainly, by the British but organised on the ground by a dedicated Communist leader, Chin Peng.

Chin Peng's forces harried the Japanese relentlessly from early 1943 to 1945, then hid their weapons until it became clear that the British had re-established their pre-war colonial presence and showed no sign of leaving. Granting independence to Malaya was complicated by the fact that although the country contained millions of Chinese, it also contained millions of Malay who, while wanting independence, did not want Chinese Communist domination to follow the departure of the British. Indeed, when the British did depart, the Federation of Malaysia they left behind had a very brief life before splitting into largely Chinese Singapore and mainly Malay Malaya.

The jungle war which preceded independence lasted for ten years and cost a great many lives – British, Chinese and Malay. The basic aim of the British and Commonwealth forces was to eliminate the Communist guerrillas, or 'CTs' as they were called, who could strike out at will from bases deep in the jungle. To find and eliminate these well-hidden bases the army formed the SAS 'Malaya Scouts' in 1950.

The Malaya Scouts were raised by Lt-Col J. M. (Mike) Calvert, a famous jungle soldier of World War II, who had also been commanding SAS troops in the final months in Germany. Calvert raised the Malaya Scouts from the regiments of the Hong Kong garrison, recruiting in the process a remarkable soldier, Major J. M. Woodhouse, who soon became famous in SAS circles not only for his fighting ability but also for his highly original methods of handling and training the men. One story goes that once, when a soldier fired his rifle by mistake, Woodhouse quietly took the rifle from him, handing him in exchange a primed grenade with the pin out. 'Hold on to that for a week,' he said, 'and then we'll give you back your rifle.'

It cannot be said that the troops who volunteered for the Malaya Scouts were all of the highest quality. There were many good, experienced fighting soldiers certainly, but there were also many misfits, and the unit suffered numerous discipline problems before the bad elements were weeded out and sent packing.

The Malaya Scouts were formed in Malaya in 1950, and after a brief period of jungle training began operations in the deep jungle, where their inexperience was compensated for, to some extent, by the assistance of Iban native trackers from Borneo. The Ibans were reported to be headhunters in their homeland, but they soon struck up close friendships with the British, often inviting British soldiers back to their longhouses, from which the troops would return bearing strange tales and fearful tattoos.

Apart from the terrorists, the main hazards of the jungle were leeches, ants, hornets, malarial mosquitoes, the occasional snake or tiger, and panics induced by wild pigs which could suddenly crash about alarmingly in the jungle beside the tracks. Soldiering in the jungle, or 'ulu', is very hard work in enervating heat, with a thick, thorny undergrowth to fight through, and steep, slippery game trails leading up steep mountains or into malarial swamps. Nevertheless, the British soldier is ever-adaptable and the Malaya Scouts soon began to know the jungle and to kill terrorists. In 1952 Calvert's men were joined by volunteers from 21 SAS and shortly afterwards the Malaya Scouts became 22 SAS.

The two big specialities of the SAS in Malaya were, first, parachuting into the jungle, thereby getting into terrorist strongholds quickly and quietly without days of slogging through the 'ulu', and, second, the development of a 'hearts and minds' campaign, to convince the jungle dwellers and the native people that the British were both helpful and friendly. This involved learning native languages, offering medical help and living with the local people to provide them with protection.

The theory was that the parachutists would crash down through the trees, but their chutes would snag on the upper branches. Each man was therefore equipped with 100 feet or so of rope with which to abseil the rest of the way to the ground. Tree-jumping looked and was very dangerous and usually resulted in at least one serious injury among the group, but the SAS used this technique until the end of the Emergency in 1958, though the widespread introduction of helicopters in 1954 rendered the practice largely unnecessary. Before that happy time though, the SAS often parachuted into action and carried the war to the terrorists even in the deepest jungle.

One of the most difficult SAS operations in tracking down the guerrillas commenced in February 1958, near the coast of the Malacca Strait in the state of Selangor. Thirty-seven men of D Squadron 22 SAS parachuted into the Telok Anson swamp, an area of marsh and jungle covering around 200 square miles. Their task was to locate and attack two groups of terrorists led by one, Ah Hoi, known to the army as 'Baby Killer' after he had murdered a pregnant woman by holding her down on a table and cutting her open with a knife before a group of terrified villagers. Such tactics helped to cow the native population but won the CTs few friends.

As tree-jumping was now rightly regarded as hazardous, no training jumps were allowed. The SAS dropped unrehearsed from a Beverley into the swamp area and began with one serious casualty when the canopy of one man's parachute failed to catch on the branches of the trees. The chute collapsed and the man fell like a lump of lead to the ground, breaking his back. Clearly this casualty had to be evacuated and trees were quickly felled to make a clearing where a helicopter could come in to hover while the injured man was secured to a stretcher and winched on board. This done, the remaining troopers, commanded by Lieutenant Harry Thompson, set out to track down the enemy.

The search for Ah Hoi led the SAS along rivers and through deep swamp water, where at times they were up to their necks and subjected to attacks by leeches and malarial mosquitoes. They soon came across traces of camps which the terrorists had recently left but it was also soon evident that Ah Hoi and his men had seen the parachutes and knew they were now being pursued. The SAS had to find and encircle Ah Hoi's band, and so one group followed the banks of the Tengi River through the swamp, reporting progress by radio to Thompson at squadron headquarters, while another group under a Sergeant Sandilands swung wide to cut across the terrorists' trail, moving cautiously through the swamp, usually under cover of darkness.

After seven days of relentless pursuit, Sandilands' patrol observed two terrorists across a stretch of swamp. Sandilands and his corporal edged nearer, neck-deep in the water, in order to get a closer look, and when they were within 50 yards of the CTs, Sandilands opened fire, killing one of the terrorists. The second man escaped into the jungle. Sandilands' troop followed his trail next day to find another freshly abandoned camp, but again Ah Hoi had fled.

Harry Thompson had moved his men to a position on the river Tengi upstream from another SAS troop, while a complete infantry cordon was placed round the outside of the swamp. Barbed wire was laid down at possible escape points along the coast. Helicopters flew in supplies of food for the SAS and hovered over the open areas searching for signs of Ah Hoi. Meanwhile, inside the swamp, the SAS continued to patrol until, after almost three weeks in these appalling conditions, many men of D Squadron were suffering from the effects of this seemingly endless life in the swamp.

Two days after the infantry cordon had finally closed around the swamp, a tiny, half-starved woman in a dark green Communist uniform approached an infantry and police checkpoint in a paddy-field. She had been sent by Ah Hoi, who had a proposition to make to the security forces. He wanted a payment of £3500 made to each of his group still in the field and an amnesty declared for those who had already been captured and were awaiting trial. The woman was told to return to Ah Hoi with the message that his proposition was unacceptable; he could either surrender within the next 24 hours or face death from the SAS or the soldiers waiting around the swamp for him to emerge. If necessary, the RAF were ready to sweep the area with bombs and rockets and force Ah Hoi out of his hiding place.

As it grew dark on the same day Ah Hoi and a handful of his men appeared from the jungle. He chose to go into exile in China rather than to prison, and so still protesting that 'the Reds would win in the end', he was sent on his way to China. It is hard not to wonder why he was not given a brief trial and a well deserved hanging.

The woman messenger took Harry Thompson and some of the SAS back into the swamp, where a further group of Ah Hoi's men were said to be ready to surrender. The route this woman courier had used for years involved swimming along a river barely 300 yards from a police post. Now, she was suffering from beri-beri and before they reached the remainder of Ah Hoi's men, she had to give up, weak with exhaustion. The remnants of Ah Hoi's group finally surrendered two days later.

British SAS soldiers soon joined up with other SAS

troops from Fiji, New Zealand and Rhodesia, and developed quite extraordinary skills, both in tracking the terrorists and in not leaving any evidence of their whereabouts behind to attract CT ambushes. They learned to move their position after dark, to give up smoking and shaving (which attracted mosquitoes and the keen noses of the terrorists), and to shoot accurately from short range at the most fleeting targets. One expert British tracker was SAS Sergeant Turnbull, who could also shoot exceptionally fast and accurately and had gained a fluent command of the Malay language.

When tracking, Turnbull didn't miss a thing, and could move stealthily through the deepest swamp and jungle while leaving no evidence of his passing. His favourite weapon was a repeater shotgun, the ideal weapon for the close-quarter, split-second fighting which the jungle contacts offered. One day, while Turnbull was leading an SAS patrol south-east of Legap, they bumped into a terrorist who appeared suddenly from the jungle, about twenty yards distant. Turnbull jerked his shotgun into his shoulder and fired with such speed that the first three shots made one continuous report. Before the sound of his shots had rattled away among the trees, Turnbull was standing over the body of the terrorist who turned out to be an important Communist organiser.

The SAS did not play a major part in the long years of the Malayan Emergency and their role, though effective, was always a minor one. In the ten years' fighting, the Communist terrorists lost over 6000 men and over 3000 were captured or surrendered, but much of this was due to solid patrol work by the Brigade of Gurkhas, to such infantry units as the Suffolk Regiment, the Scots Guards or the units of the 3rd Commando Brigade, Royal Marines, or to aerial bombing. The SAS's main role was the cutting of Communist supply lines, the protection of the local people from intimidation, and the offer of eventual independence.

The Emergency was, however, highly important to the SAS. The campaign brought the regiment back into being, and provided it with a role. In the swamps and jungles of the peninsula, the SAS relearned their craft, re-established their reputation and prepared them for other, even harder tasks in the years ahead.

9

WAR IN THE OMAN
1958–72

The SAS killed 108 hardcore Communist terrorists during their ten-year stint in Malaya; not a large score perhaps, but a useful one. To the SAS the long campaign in Malaya provided many long term benefits. They became accepted as an established unit in the 'peacetime' British army, though since the 'peacetime' British army was always fighting somewhere this adjective indicated only a theoretical state of calm. The post-Malaya conflicts also marked another use for the SAS, a period when the regiment fought not as a unit but in different roles, in various countries and most often in small squadron-sized detachments, making up in effectiveness what they lacked in size.

The SAS believed then, and still believe today, that adaptability is the key to their survival. As the Emergency began to peter out in 1958, the regiment found a new field of activity in a very different kind of terrain, among the deserts and jebels of Arabia, in the Sultanate of Oman. The Oman has changed a lot since the SAS first fought there. In 1958 it was ruled by Sultan Sa'id, a despotic ruler who kept Oman firmly in his grasp in an atmosphere reminiscent of the Middle Ages – a state of affairs which caused unrest among the people and fostered revolt. Sa'id was overthrown in 1970 by his son Qaboos, a much more enlightened man (Sandhurst-educated), who has, in the years since 1970, transformed the country into one of the happier Arab nations.

Oil is the dynamic of modern Arabia, the basic reason

for the region's strategic and economic importance. Arabia is also an area where influence rather than direct pressure is the key to diplomatic success, a place where even if the steel fist is barely concealed by the velvet glove, a certain delicacy is still required, even in the more blatant kind of power politics. For such low-key manoeuvres, the small but hard-hitting units of the SAS are often ideal tools, and they learned how to conduct their craft in the troubled state of Oman.

The Sultanate of Muscat and Oman, with the Trucial Oman States to the north, occupies a commanding position in Arabia – overlooking the tanker routes through the Gulf of Oman and the Persian Gulf, the sea lane to the rich oilfields of Saudia Arabia, Kuwait, Bahrain and Iran. To keep the Oman pro-Western was the prime role of British forces in the years between 1957 and 1976, a period when the SAS spread their squadrons between the Oman, the fighting in Aden, and the confrontation in Borneo. The SAS involvement in Oman fell into two main phases: from 1958–9 in the Jabal Akhdar, and much later and more deeply, from 1970–6 in the south-western province of Dhufar. The first SAS unit arrived in the Oman from Malaya in November 1958, and began operations with a brief, sharp struggle with a rebellious sheik, the Sultan of the Jabal Akhdar, the Lord of the Green Mountain.

The Jabal Akhdar is a high fertile plateau set some 3000 metres above the humid coastal plain. The British forces supporting Sultan Sa'id had already tried to storm the Jabal in battalion strength and been driven off with losses. As soon as D Squadron 22 SAS arrived in the area, they came face to face with its dangers. One soldier on temporary attachment from the Army Medical Corps was blown up on two separate occasions and finally had to be evacuated by helicopter as the tracks were constantly mined. Another soldier, an experienced SAS corporal who had won a Military Medal in Malaya, was killed by a single shot from a sniper while walking the slopes of the Jabal.

It was therefore decided to move onto the Jabal only at night, unless the urgency of the situation dictated otherwise. Guided by a rather frightened sheik, an SAS troop ascended the north side of the Jabal Akhdar, a slope dotted with enemy 'sangars' or stone-built emplacements, which were fortunately unmanned. Led by Captain Walker, the SAS occupied these sangars, within machine-gun range of a strong rebel post at Aqbat al Dhafar. It wasn't long before they came under heavy fire by guerrillas armed with rifles and automatic weapons who began to advance towards them. The SAS moved into position on a forward slope and held fire until the enemy was a hundred yards away. Then their barrage of Bren and rifle fire swept the slope, killing or wounding a number of the enemy and forcing the others to disperse.

At the end of December, Captain Walker led two SAS troops in an attack against a twin-peaked mountain, code-named 'Sabrina'. Just before the troops reached the top of the hill they were observed by the enemy, who promptly opened fire. Captain Walker hauled himself up a sheer cliff by rope and hurled a grenade over the top which killed one of the guerrillas, whereupon the remainder fled into the rocks. In the confused hand-to-hand fighting which followed the SAS killed a further eight guerrillas.

While all this was going on, a small patrol on the south side of 'Sabrina' had observed a cave used by the guerrillas to guard the tracks leading up the south face of the Jabal Akhdar. This cave was believed to be the main store for rebel weapons and ammunition. Two nights later two SAS troops moved in to destroy it. One group moved through enemy territory for ten hours so that they could approach the cave undetected. Taking cover 200 metres from the entrance they covered it with a loaded 3.5-inch rocket-launcher.

The only position from which they would fire this weapon was directly below the cave, which meant that the rocket crew had to kneel up or stand, in full view of the defenders in order to obtain a hit, and the near slopes contained many small caves where enemy snipers could be hiding. When one of the guerrillas came out of the mouth of the cave at first light, the SAS opened fire, showering the entrance with rockets, rifle and machine-gun fire. The fire-fight lasted for over an hour, and as the rebels were driven back, involved mortars and air support from rocket-firing Venom fighters of the Sultan's air force. SAS operations in the Oman may have been small scale, but they often involved all arms.

By the end of December it had become evident that the D Squadron's position on the north side of the Akhdar plateau needed strengthening. By this time, although a total of 40 rebels had been killed, the SAS patrols were meeting with ever more determined resistance. They would need the strength of a full squadron if they were to gain the plateau, while a further squadron strength force would be needed to keep up pressure on another front and disperse or distract the enemy, who always outnumbered the SAS and had the advantage of defending prepared positions.

Commanded by David Stirling's wartime driver, now Major John Cooper, A Squadron 22 SAS arrived in early January, and set about the task of again attacking the twin-peaked 'Sabrina' mountain, which offered the main gateway to the enemy position. The first few days were spent patrolling on the north side of the plateau in an endeavour to delude the rebels into thinking that this area would be the main route for the British attack. A similar hoax was launched from Tanuf, eight miles from 'Sabrina', and the deception plan here was backed up by 'confidentially' informing four local donkey-drivers, whose animals were to carry ammunition, that Tanuf would be the main assault route. The donkey-drivers were threatened with dire consequences if they disclosed the secret, and the information therefore reached the rebels within the day.

While these deception plans were being carried out in an effort to disperse the rebels, a small troop which had been quietly patrolling the north side secretly rejoined the rest of D Squadron for the main attack. The Sultan's chief of staff, together with the commanding officer of 22 SAS,

Colonel Deane-Drummond, and his two Squadron Commanders, Majors Watts and Cooper, had examined detailed aerial photographs of the region, and it was decided to move directly up to the Jabal along a steep ridge leading from lower ground held by the Sultan's army. This meant a nine-hour night climb, at one point ascending a 1500 metre cliff with ropes. Each SAS soldier had to carry a minimum of 30 kilos in equipment and ammunition. Close behind the SAS squadron came a troop of the Life Guards serving as infantry, and a company of the Sultan's Northern Frontier Regiment, complete with donkeys carrying their Vickers machine-guns.

The first men to climb the Jabal were about three-quarters of the way up when they came across a Browning .5-inch machine-gun, but whoever should have been manning it must have withdrawn to the heights above, believing their position was safe. The rest of the way seemed clear, and therefore Colonel Deane-Drummond, moving with the forward troop, decided that they should dump their Bergen rucksacks and make a dash for the top carrying only the minimum of ammunition. Armed with rifles and whatever ammunition they could carry on them, the SAS began the steep ascent to the high plateau of the Jabal.

At dawn an air strike by Venoms and a parachute supply drop on the south side convinced the guerrillas that an airborne attack on the area was beginning. The rebels fled, leaving behind them eight 3-inch mortars, a number of Brens, a large number of mines, various quantities of ammunition, together with a number of documents of great interest to the intelligence services.

The arrival of SAS troops on the Jabal Akhdar effectively ended the rebellion of the Lord of the Green Mountain, and the first phase of the SAS operations in Oman. It was a neat, low-key operation, described by *The Times* as 'a brilliant example of economy in the use of force'.

Unfortunately, British influence in the Oman did not extend much beyond the role of providing periodic provision of muscle. Sultan Sa'id remained in power, still a total despot, the country still remained medieval and those who were rich enough or intelligent enough soon fled abroad to more liberal climes. The people suffered and rebellion prospered, notably in the mountainous southern province of Dhufar, which lay on the border with the Communist-controlled republic of South Yemen. Sultan Sa'id survived numerous assassination attempts and was finally overthrown in 1970 by his son, Sultan Qaboos who, with help from the West, eventually transformed the Oman into one of the most pleasant and progressive Arab states. Qaboos entered into his dangerous inheritance with revolt simmering everywhere, most notably in the province of Dhufar. He sent at once for the assistance of the SAS, who began a campaign which combined a version of their Malayan 'hearts and minds' operations with military training for the Sultan's disaffected and dispirited forces, the irregular bands known as *firqas*. SAS teams training the *firqas* contained Arab-speakers who were ready and willing to fight with and for their charges as, for example, at Mirbat, in the summer of 1972.

In mid-July, the group of ten SAS making up the British army training team in Mirbat, all soldiers from B Squadron, were preparing to leave for England. They had just spent three months in Mirbat, a drab little cantonment which boasted no more than a group of flat-roofed houses and two old, mud-walled forts. It was enclosed on two sides by the sea and lay more than 40 miles away from the provincial capital of Dhufar, Salalah. Although officially a training camp, Mirbat was still in the front line, in so far as there was one. The SAS had seen a little action while there, days or nights punctuated by the occasional crash of a mortar bomb or the sudden arrival of an anti-tank missile; during the last week of May and the first week of June alone, a total of twelve mortar bombs had fallen on the town, followed by three 74 mm shells. Life in Mirbat was sometimes busy, often boring, and occasionally dangerous.

The British army training team, known as BATmen, had spent the time training the local *firqas* and generally fostering goodwill among the locals. Looming up in the heat haze to the north was the long bulk of the mountains, and here in mid-July, a large group of Communist-backed rebels from the so-called Dhufar Liberation Front assembled for a swift *coup-de-main* against the Sultan's *firqa* and their British advisers in the garrison at Mirbat.

While the SAS were packing or turning in to their sleeping-bags on the night of 18 July, the guerrillas were moving forward ready for the start of their heaviest assault of the ten-year war. The rebels had gathered more than 250 of their best men for this attack, well armed with Russian Kalashnikov AK47 automatic rifles, grenades, machine-guns, mortars, 75 mm anti-tank guns and Swedish rocket launchers. The guerrillas marched south, heading down towards Mirbat, and once off the Jabal, divided into smaller groups of ten, fanning out into a wide circle to surround the town. Others went on past the town to the sea and fanned out along the coast to attack the town from that side. It was a good plan and before dawn the unsuspecting garrison was surrounded.

The garrison of Mirbat consisted of some 30 Askaris from northern Oman, armed with obsolescent British .303-inch rifles. These were the town's watchkeepers and occupied a fort close to the beach known as the Wali's Fort. Inside the town itself, were the local *firqa*, whom the SAS were training, a force of about 40 men with a further twenty away carrying out recce work in the mountains, armed with FN.762 automatic rifles and light machine-guns. There was a further force of around 25 men of the Dhufar gendarmerie, also armed with FN rifles and a single light machine-gun, positioned in a second fort just inside the enclave occupied by the SAS training team. A British Second World War 25-pounder field gun was positioned in front of this fort, which overlooked the town and the town's single airstrip. Other than the 25-pounder, the only heavy weapons available to the defence were a single .50-inch Browning machine-gun and an 81 mm mortar.

On a hill about half a mile to the north of the town, another eight gendarmes were on sentry duty, and it was this position which first came under attack by the rebels. The rebels crept up on this outpost just before dawn, but they were spotted by the gendarmes, who challenged them and got off a single shot before the rebel assault line swept in. Four of the gendarmes were killed in the ensuing fight, but the remaining four managed to escape and raised the alarm.

Having lost that essential element of surprise, the rebels began their main attack by opening a rapid mortar fire on the forts and the town. The SAS returned fire with the 81 mm mortar, and their white phosphorous smoke soon wafted out obscuring their positions from the enemy's view. Another SAS trooper opened fire with the .50 Browning, covering the area between the two forts, while other SAS men took on scattered groups of advancing rebels. Although the defence leapt into action quickly, they were still scattered and outnumbered at least five to one. Captain Kealy, commanding the SAS, sent an urgent message for reinforcements to the provincial headquarters at Salalah, and established radio contact with his heaviest weapon, the 25-pounder crew in action in front of the fort. With this in action, and every weapon firing, the fight for Mirbat really got under way.

Rebel troops had by now advanced into the town and bursts of machine-gun fire were raking the streets; mortar bombs were crashing all around the forts and enemy bullets whistling in from the seaward side. The garrison was completely surrounded and fighting back to beat off attacks from every direction. The SAS mortar crew were stuffing bombs down the barrel, engaging any group large enough to engage, while the training team in the fort were using every weapon available. The 25-pounder outside the fort was being manned by an Omani gunner Walid Khamis, and two Fijian SAS men who had dashed from the fort at the beginning of the attack to serve as loaders, slamming shells into the breech, leaping clear as the big gun fired.

The rebels were now suffering heavy casualties but still pressed home their attack; as one group was hit another came forward to take its place. Gradually they gained ground until they were within yards of the inner perimeter fence, where they opened fire on the fort with their Soviet RPG-7 rockets and a Carl Gustav grenade launcher. The Carl Gustav's powerful 84 mm rockets soon had a shattering effect on the fort. The tower collapsed but the SAS team continued firing their mortar, the .50 Browning and light machine-guns, and now turned their fire on the leading groups of rebels, who were approaching the perimeter and about to rush the fort. The battle for Mirbat had reached a critical moment.

Captain Kealy was still maintaining his radio link with the gun crew in front of the fort and also with the Sultan's *firqa* in their fort by the beach, but at this stage every group could only hold its own position. Kealy had asked Salalah to stand by with strike aircraft, but now the billowing smoke together with low cloud conditions made it unlikely the the air force would be able to get in.

The rebels broke through the wire but still could not succeed in overrunning the fort. Becoming concerned about the lack of return fire from the gendarmerie fort and the field-gun opposition, Kealy decided to go out there himself. This involved a 300 metre dash over exposed ground under heavy enemy fire. Others in the SAS training team volunteered to go with him, but in the event he took only one man, his medical orderly, trooper Tobin.

Kealy and his medical orderly ran in short dashes covered by fire from the Browning and the light machine-guns. Moving through the smoke, one firing cover while the other advanced, they eventually reached the 25-pounder gun position, where they found the Oman artillery gunner lying seriously wounded. On the parapet of the fort they found a dead soldier lying across his machine-gun and another dead gendarme in the gun pit. Both Fijian SAS men were continuing to fight, although one was bleeding badly from a head wound while the other was trying to stop the flow of blood from a wound on his face as he continued to load and fire the 25-pounder, which was now fully depressed and firing point blank into the still-advancing enemy.

From the bunker Kealy sent a sharp radio message calling for an air strike and just as he had sent it, the gallant Fijian operating the 25-pounder was shot dead. Shortly afterwards Tobin had the lower part of his face shot away, so that the gun position was now manned by Kealy and one wounded Fijian. The rebels were less than 30 yards away.

With the gun position and the fort behind it under heavy fire from small arms and the Carl Gustav, Kealy picked off one rebel just about to fire, then shot another who was running in towards their position with grenades. The Fijian managed to prop himself up on one elbow and fire at the rebel line sweeping in from the left flank. Then a rebel light machine-gun started spraying their trench, bullets cracking close across the top of their heads, forcing them to take cover. Now came the grenades, exploding quite close but missing their target. One rolled into the gun pit but failed to go off.

Just as their position became hopeless, two Strikemaster jets of the Sultan's air force roared close overhead, almost at ground level. Kealy passed target details over his radio and 500-pound bombs rained down where the rebels were gathering for their last decisive push. The battle around the fort and gun position had been raging for an hour and a half as the second wave of Strikemasters came in. One of these knocked out the rebel machine-guns on the slopes of the Jabal Ali, which overlooked the town, while another attacked the rebels hiding near the fort and the perimeter, with cannon and machine-gun fire.

The air strikes provided a breathing space, but it was evident that substantial ground reinforcements would be required to resolve the situation. Fortunately the replacement training team from G Squadron 22 SAS had arrived the previous day at Salalah. When Kealy's request for assistance arrived at the base the men in G Squadron were checking their weapons on the local firing range. They flew in by helicopter directly to Mirbat beach, arriving under cover of the second air strike. The first helicopter lift of 18 SAS troopers moved inland in two groups, knocking out a rebel position on a ridge overlooking the town. This new SAS assault group was soon spotted by rebels near the fort, who opened fire before they withdrew. Meanwhile the second helicopter lift was landing near the beach and engaging the rebel positions on the southern and seaward side of the town. Before long the rebels were in full retreat, driven back to the Jabal by the *firqa*.

By mid-morning the battle was over and the most serious casualties had been lifted out by the helicopter, with the wounded Fijian insisting on walking out to the aircraft. The defenders' total casualties turned out to be mercifully small: four dead and three wounded – while the rebel body count was at least 30 dead and ten wounded.

The attack on Mirbat was the largest assault mounted by the Dhufari rebels and they never recovered from this defeat or attempted a similar assault again.

Kealy was later awarded the DSO for this epic defence, and Trooper Tobin, who died of his wounds, received a posthumous DCM. Captain Kealy, by then a major, died from exposure in 1979 while taking part in an SAS exercise in the Brecon Beacons.

10

THE BATTLE FOR BORNEO
1963–6

Malaya became independent in 1957, after which, as we have seen in the last chapter, some of the SAS squadrons departed to fresh fields in the Arabian Gulf. It was still necessary to provide military aid to the new nation in order to combat the two or three thousand Communist guerrillas still roaming the jungle and, by rotating their squadrons, the SAS managed to keep their jungle fighting skills well honed until they were once again required. This opportunity came in Borneo between 1963 and 1966.

After Malayan independence had been declared there was a pause of two years before the federation disintegrated. Singapore became independent in 1959, and in 1963 Malaya and Singapore joined with the state of Sabah in what was then Borneo, to form the short-lived Federation of Malaysia. All three states have since separated and are now completely independent, but before that, there was trouble from Indonesia.

The foundation of the federation was viewed with hostility by the nearby Republic of Indonesia. The islands of Indonesia virtually encircle Malaya and Borneo, sweeping around them in a wide loop from north-west to southeast, each island of that long chain offering the perfect launching pad for infiltrators. The 'confrontation' never developed into all-out war, but there was plenty of stiff jungle fighting.

The main engagements of the 'confrontation' took place in the jungles of Borneo, along the frontiers of three formerly British protectorates, Sabah, Brunei and Sarawak, which the Brooke family had handed over to Britain in 1946. Britain felt obliged to aid this new state's resistance to Indonesian attack, so by February 1963 SAS troopers, Gurkhas and the Royal Marine commandos were patrolling the 900 mile frontier with Indonesia.

The word 'confrontation' may give rise to the idea that this campaign was more a matter of belligerent statements than actual fighting, but this is far from the case. The British, Malayan and Gurkha forces were frequently under attack and often outnumbered by well trained regular units of the Indonesian army. It may have been called 'confrontation', but to the people at the sharp end it more frequently resembled a war. Take, for example, the following SAS patrol action in Borneo.

A patrol of 22 SAS was coming down from a ridge along a track which led towards an Indonesian border post which their scouts had spotted the previous day. This post appeared to have been vacated months before, but as the leading trooper approached it and ducked under some bamboo, he spotted an Indonesian soldier a few metres to his flank. In the exchange of fire he was hit in the thigh and fell into a clump of bamboo almost on top of yet another Indonesian soldier, whom he shot and killed. The Indonesian soldiers in the ambush were now engaging the SAS from well concealed positions and the patrol's commander, a Sergeant Lillico, lay on the track, wounded in the first firing and unable to move. He could still use his rifle and returned the enemy fire while the others in the patrol took cover.

The bullet in the leading trooper's thigh had shattered the bone, so also unable to walk, he hopped back to join Lillico, who ordered him to return up the track and bring the rest of the patrol forward. Meanwhile Sergeant Lillico dragged himself back up the ridge and opened fire in the direction of the enemy post. Shortly after this the Indonesians withdrew, possibly under the misapprehension that SAS reinforcements would be moving in to surround their positions.

The remainder of the patrol had decided to withdraw to the nearest infantry post, pick up reinforcements and return next day to search the area for their wounded colleagues. By the morning of the second day the injured trooper had managed to cover half the distance back to the infantry camp, dragging himself painfully along the ground before he was found by the search party.

Meanwhile, Sergeant Lillico had managed to gain the top of the ridge, some 300 metres from where he had been hit. The single shots he fired to attract the attention of the search party were answered by bursts of machine-gun fire from the enemy close by. Lillico could hear the noise of a helicopter overhead, but dared not risk showing himself while the enemy were still searching for him. He lay up all day and was spotted by the helicopter when it returned during the evening. He was winched out, a day and a half after he had been injured in that first fierce exchange of fire.

The confrontation was not fought against ragged, ill-equipped guerrillas but against a well-equipped enemy, operating in company sized groups of 80 or more men, with heavy weapons, machine-guns and mortars. The average size of an SAS patrol was four men. These Indonesian companies would fight hard when contacted and when forced to retreat lay ambushes to trap their pursuers. This led to the 'shoot and scoot' policy, where after making a contact and a brief exchange of fire, the SAS would break off the engagement, radio for reinforcements, often Gurkhas, and then dog the enemy's footsteps until they could be brought to battle. 'Shoot and scoot' kept the casualties down but did not always work. Fortunately, on those occasions when 'push' became 'shove', the SAS could give a good account of themselves.

Lieutenant Skardon, an Australian attached to the SAS, had been with his patrol for just four weeks when they first had a contact. Sensing enemy presence in the close, dead ground near to their camp, Lieutenant Skardon and three others decided to investigate. Finding nothing unusual close by they set out next morning to check the main track parallel to the river. The jungle was quiet as the four men crossed the river and climbed to the track on the ridge, but they sensed that all was not as it should be. They proceeded with extreme caution, slipping from one cover to another, until one of the patrol almost fell over an Indonesian soldier kneeling behind a tree. He was dealt with immediately with one shot. Indonesian fire now came in on them from every side, a sprung ambush, and the scout gave the order to get out and clear of the area. Lieutenant Skardon moved back with two troopers, but Trooper White, who had killed the Indonesian soldier, stayed behind to cover them, opening fire on a platoon of enemy soldiers who had by now appeared along the ridge above.

The ground here was very open and White was soon hit and wounded. Disregarding the 'shoot and scoot' policy, Skardon ran back up the slope and joined White, dragging him behind a large tree. From there, still under very heavy enemy fire, Skardon pulled White into a hollow, hoping it would cover them, but the enemy were now flooding down the slope and their continuous fire was even breaking branches from the trees, which were falling down all around them. Skardon saw that the blood had stopped flowing from the gaping wound in White's thigh and feared that he was already dead, so decided to get him down to the shelter of the riverbank. He started down again on the hazardous journey, dragging or carrying White, dashing from hollow to hollow, still pursued by intense but, fortunately, inaccurate fire.

A group of the enemy had by now moved in towards the creek from the flank, cutting off Skardon's only hope of escape. Then he realised that White had indeed died, so, leaving his body, Skardon fired at the enemy heading for the river and made a dash for it himself. Once into it he was out of view behind the high banks. It was now necessary to move off downstream and quickly, towards better cover on the far bank, before being cut off. He reached some thick undergrowth and hauled himself up the bank into cover and safety.

Next day, an SAS troop and Gurkhas swept through the area to recover White's body. Nearby lay the body of the Indonesian soldier White had shot, and higher on the ridge, the vacated positions for over 30 enemy soldiers, each littered with empty cartridge cases.

Not all operations require skills in close-quarter combat. The SAS Regiment retains an intelligence-gathering capacity where stealth may be as effective as gunplay, even if the one may sometimes lead to the other, as D Squadron found out during an operation near Sidut across the Indonesian border. Their task was to capture a man who had the habit of visiting a certain hut, and bring him and/or his papers back across the border for inspection.

A company of the Scots Guards secured a crossing over the river which marked the border, and the SAS crossed here at dusk. After a cautious approach march they stopped for the night within a few yards of the hut. As dawn broke they moved stealthily forward, half pleased to see tripwire attached to a mortar bomb fuse; clearly this was a worthwhile target. They surrounded the hut, but just as they were about to move in, a small boy came out and walked towards them. Seeing the SAS, he hurried back, yelling, and the enemy reaction was rapid. Someone burst out onto the verandah of the hut, grabbing a weapon, but was shot dead by the SAS before he could fire it. The SAS dashed in firing as they went, but the occupants of the hut ran out of the back door and into the dense jungle before the SAS could shoot them down.

A grenade was lobbed into the hut, which produced another Indonesian soldier, and then the SAS moved inside, where they found ammunition, rifles, grenades and all manner of equipment – and in lieu of the prisoner, documents, which were safely delivered to the intelligence people.

One way in which the SAS differs from other troops, is that they are an aggressor force. In most situations the British army labours under the problem that the enemy is supposed to fire first, but the SAS can and do seek out the opposition, and carry the battle to an unsuspecting enemy.

One such aggressive operation was undertaken by SAS Corporal Carter and his patrol. After a tip-off they went to recce an area on the Koemba river where two 'recently built' huts had shown up in aerial photographs. The huts were found to be old and of no consequence, but many local boats seemed to be continually passing on the river so the patrol established an observation post on the bank. Some of these passing craft carried Indonesian soldiers and military supplies for the enemy base at Siding so, having observed the situation for a few days, Corporal Carter decided to put a spoke in the wheel. On the sixth day a boat came down from Siding crewed by three soldiers with their weapons in the bottom of the boat, just out of reach.

When they were within easy range, Carter shot the centre soldier dead. The remaining two were knocked over the side by bullets from the other members of the patrol. One of these died instantly, and a grenade in the water finished off the last man. This sudden eruption of SAS activity in their Siding supply route gave little comfort to the enemy.

Neither were all 'confrontation' incidents small affairs involving a handful of combatants. On one occasion a large force of at least 150 well trained Indonesian soldiers, backed by two further regular army companies, attacked Plaman Mapu on the Sarawak front. When the attack came, the main part of the defending force from B Company, 2 Para were out in the nearby jungle searching for signs of the enemy, and it was left to those remaining to hold the base camp, fighting hand to hand against odds with whatever weapons they could snatch up. The company sergeant-major was blinded in one eye during the battle, but so inspired the men, who were mostly cooks and drivers from company headquarters, that over 30 Indonesian casualties were counted against British losses of two killed and eight wounded.

Deep reconnaissance behind enemy lines is never without risk. Captain Robin Letts and his patrol were given the task of finding more about the enemy's lines of communication several miles inside the Indonesian border.

Getting to their observation point involved slow and careful infiltration through deep jungle and swamp, but after a week they were established in a good spot overlooking one of those rivers which, in the absence of good roads, provide the main means of communication in Indonesia. Letts established a two-man watch on the river at a point where it formed a bend, offering a clear view up and down the river, 60 metres to the left and 30 metres to the right. During the evening they watched several enemy boats pass downstream, with two armed soldiers in each, and Letts radioed back to base for permission to engage the enemy should the opportunity occur.

By the following morning, no permission to attack had been received, but Letts decided to engage the enemy anyway, and at close quarters if possible. The river was evidently a main water route, both for men and supplies heading for the front. It was also likely that there was a staging point in the village nearby and therefore the enemy's reaction to any ambush would be quick.

Having noted that boats negotiating the bend had to come close to the shore, as dawn broke Letts took a look around the bank for a likely ambush position. Letts had also noticed that as soon as a boat had passed the bend it could no longer be seen by those behind, so any second boat would be unable to support the crew of the boat in front. Having found a good spot, Letts took up his position at the top of the bend with one man on his right and two men on his left, so as to cover boats coming from either direction. The enemy would hit the ambush when the leading boat rounded the bend, opposite the outside man on the far side.

Letts expected that they would have to deal with a maximum of eight enemy soldiers in four boats, and for the patrol of four SAS, this was considered reasonable odds, particularly as they had the element of surprise on their side. However, having sprung their ambush and aroused the enemy they would then have to get back through miles of difficult and hostile territory. All in all, this ambush took a considerable amount of nerve.

After two and a half hours of waiting, a boat was sighted on the left, but containing not two but three soldiers and a second boat followed a length behind, also containing three soldiers. The front two in each craft were paddling, but the third man was alert and watching the banks, his rifle ready. Then, just as the SAS were about to open fire, a third boat appeared. The odds were getting shorter.

As the first boat came round the bend, the second boat, badly handled, crashed into the bank almost at the spot where an SAS man lay hidden. Fortunately the crew's attention was taken up with manoeuvring the boat and they did not see him, while the leading boat moved around the top of the bend and drew level with the SAS man. The second boat drifted past the outer man and Letts stood up ready to fire at the sentry in the stern, but the bowman saw him and, reacting with amazing dexterity, dropped his paddle and snatched up his rifle. The outer SAS trooper shot him full in the chest, sending the man crashing overboard, while Letts and the other SAS trooper faced five of the enemy at close range. Letts shot the rear man in the first boat, sending him reeling against the gunwale. The second boat's crew flipped their boat and disappeared under the water, with the SAS man firing a full rifle magazine into the water at the point where they disappeared.

The remaining man on the first boat fired again at Letts, who sprang sideways into cover and fired back, his shot knocking the man forward into the boat. Letts then turned back and saw the man he had just shot dragging himself up from the bottom of the bank. He shot him again, twice, killing him outright. One of the crew from the capsized boat now crawled out of the water to the bank and was taking aim at Letts when a trooper spotted him and fired first, knocking the man back into the water. A second enemy soldier dashed ashore and reached the first man's abandoned gun, but was killed before he could fire it. These Indonesian soldiers were reacting quickly and fighting with great courage.

When the first shot of the ambush was fired, the nearest SAS trooper engaged the third boat, which was heading straight for him and barely 40 metres away. First he shot the bowman, who fell overboard; then he shot the second man who also fell into the water; finally he shot at the third man, who followed his comrades into the water, which was now littered with bodies and overturned boats.

The SAS men were all standing, grasping their weapons, when yet another boat appeared, but the sound of gunfire had warned the enemy and they backpaddled frantically for shelter and slipped swiftly away, leaving eight dead soldiers in the river or lying on the blood-stained shore. The ambush, from first shot to last, had taken less than four minutes.

Letts and his party now had to get away, and they opted for a swift retreat, crashing through the jungle at speed, with mortar bombs from the enemy staging post dropping on the ambush position and Indonesian troops in hot pursuit. Letts' patrol covered the distance to the frontier in just over twelve hours, a distance they had taken a week to cross on the way in. They were finally lifted across the frontier by helicopter. For his skill and daring in this action, Letts was later awarded the Military Cross.

11

THE RADFAN 1964–7

The turbulent 1960s and 70s offered the troopers of 22 SAS plenty of action, notably in Arabia, and it would be inconceivable to leave this theatre of war without looking at one of the last colonial campaigns fought by the British army, in the colony and protectorate of Aden.

Aden is a small place, a wretched fly-blown port at the southern end of the Red Sea; one of those places which had some importance in the days of Empire when it was a coaling station on the sea road to India, and is now strategically important because of its location astride oil routes from the Persian Gulf. To the north of Aden lie the Radfan mountains, which line the frontier with the Yemen Arab Republic, while – in the 1960s – to the east lay the Communist 'Peoples' Democratic Republic of South Yemen'.

In the 1960s, hemmed in by enemies on every side, the British forces in Aden (those long-suffering infantry, the Royal Marines, Highlanders and paratroopers) fought a long and worthless campaign and gained little from it but another lot of experience and plenty of casualties. Aden was scheduled for independence in 1968, but as the Yemeni-inspired violence escalated within the colony this date was moved foward to November 1967, while all ideas of a British base there after independence were abandoned, and Aden was, for a time, a popular port for the Soviet eastern fleet.

A squadron of the SAS arrived in Aden in 1964, and

went into action almost at once in an operation in the Radfan which has since entered SAS history as the 'Edwards patrol'.

The Radfan mountains cover an area of around 400 square miles, lying to the east of the Dhala Road, and are inhabited by a group of tribes described by a commando officer as 'a xenophobic lot ... every man had been brought up from boyhood with a rifle in his hands, knowing how to use it and frequently doing so if any argument could not be settled. The arrival of the British army was seen as a chance for some target practice.'

The object of the British advance into the Radfan was to pacify these tribes and discourage them from mining the Dhala Road. The force under orders for this task consisted of 45 Commando Royal Marines, B Company, 3rd Bn, the Parachute Regiment, and A Squadron, 22 SAS. The task called for the capture of a rocky feature code named 'Cap Badge', which overlooked the main dissident stronghold, the village of Danaba. Other features by the village were code-named 'Rice Bowl', 'Coca-Cola', and 'Sand Fly'. The approach to Danaba was to be made by 45 Commando through the rough terrain of the Wadi Boran. The plan required 45 to march on 29 and 30 April, while 3 Troop of A Squadron infiltrated onto Cap Badge on the same night and secured a drop zone for a parachute drop at dawn by the men from 3 Para.

As it grew dark on 29 April, 3 Troop, led by Captain Robin Edwards and totalling ten men, set off in armoured cars for their start line in the Wadi Rabwa. Edwards' men were tough, experienced soldiers, all having seen action in Borneo and Malaya, with the exception of the signaller, an ex-Royal Engineer named Warburton.

The patrol then had to cover about eight miles on foot over difficult terrain before arriving at the drop zone. Night infiltration was usually the only safe way to get about the Radfan. In this case the darkness did not give sufficient cover and the patrol was in trouble from the start. Even as the armoured cars laboured up the Wadi Rabwa off the Dhala Road, they came under sporadic rifle and machine-gun fire. The armoured cars could only advance slowly and it soon appeared that they would have to halt completely. While armoured car gunners gave covering fire back into the hills, the Edwards patrol left the vehicles and, humping their heavy Bergens, crept quietly away into the darkness.

Having lost the advantage of surprise but avoiding casualties from enemy fire, the patrol made its way slowly through the dunes and up Wadi Rabwa, while to the right there lay the massive 1300-metre heights of their objective, Jabal Ashquab. Signaller Warburton was now suffering from severe stomach cramps and the patrol had to pause at intervals for him to catch up, but after a while it became apparent that he was getting weaker, slower and struggling to keep going. In an effort to stick to their original timing, the patrol divided and started to straggle.

Shortly after midnight, realising that they would not reach their objective by daylight, Edwards decided to halt. They were now near the top of Jabal Ashquab where there were two old rock-built sangars in which they could shelter throughout the day.

The original idea was that they should be in hiding on Cap Badge before dawn broke and stay there in hiding until dusk, when they would secure the drop zone perimeter and mark it with torches and an Aldis lamp for the parachute drop that night. They were still a good three miles away from Cap Badge and any attempt to reach it in daylight was clearly out of the question. Edwards sensibly decided to take cover in the sangars and give Warburton, who was still suffering from what seemed to be an attack of food poisoning, time to recover. They radioed their position back to the SAS squadron commander and lay up successfully for the rest of the night. Some time during the following morning their presence was detected by the tribesmen.

Within minutes armed tribesmen were pouring out from a nearby village and were climbing the rocky slope towards the sangars. The SAS opened fire, so the tribesmen took cover and began to surround them. Sporadic firing went on for about two hours as the tribesmen worked their way closer and finally onto a ridge above. Edwards had anticipated this and managed to make contact with RAF Hunter ground-strafing fighters, who flew a contact patrol over Edwards' beleaguered position.

Just as the dissidents began to assault the SAS position from the top of the ridge the first pair of Hunters swept down across the bill. This forced the tribesmen to back off but they took cover close to the sangars and opened a heavy fire. The SAS had no way out – the battle had reached stalemate. The tribesmen were firing at anything that moved and they were such good shots that the SAS were pinned down.

During the long daylight hours the Hunters continued to circle overhead but the SAS realised that the enemy was being continually reinforced and moving ever closer. The sangars were now under fire from less than 50 metres range and when it grew dark it would be impossible for the Hunters to provide air cover. The enemy knew this and were only waiting until they could rush the sangars in force.

As it grew dark Edwards was informed over the radio that the parachute drop on Cap Badge had been abandoned. They were to try and break out just after dark and make their way back to the Dhala Road. Edwards requested an artillery barrage on their position to take place at 1900 hours, hoping they would be able to escape while the barrage kept the enemy's heads down. Each man took only his rifle, ammunition and emergency rations. Two of the men had sustained leg injuries, and Signaller Warburton had died. The barrage came down on time but as they broke from the sangars a storm of rifle fire swept their position. Edwards was hit several times and fell to the ground, but the others continued their advance. As the survivors leapt into the valley the enemy continued to fire on the sangars from opposite sides, and the SAS realised that two groups of tribesmen were now shooting at each other. Keeping to the high ground, they followed the hillside round the Wadi Rabwa. The artillery barrage was still falling onto the sangars, but by this time the tribesmen had withdrawn, taking with them the bodies of Edwards and Warburton.

The patrol spent that night struggling up and down the gulleys, keeping to the high ground where possible. The two wounded men tried to keep up but from time to time everyone had to stop while the medical orderly redressed their bleeding wounds, and progress was slow.

Once off the hill they found a goat track heading in the right direction and made their way down it in single file, the two wounded men at the rear. One of them looked back, having heard a sound as if someone was following them. In the distance he saw a white clad figure on the track behind. The two wounded SAS men hid behind a nearby bush, rifles ready, and waited. The figure in white was a dissident with three more following at his heels.

As they drew near, the two SAS soldiers stepped from cover and opened fire, shooting all four dead as the rest of the SAS patrol, hearing the shooting, rushed back. They all moved off again, keeping a careful watch, and within an hour the two men at the rear were once again certain they were being followed. The patrol took over and waited. Their followers were two more dissident groups, descending from the ridge above, who also walked into the SAS ambush and were killed.

Having beaten off their immediate pursuers, the Edwards' patrol, still full of fight, continued to work their way back towards the Dhala Road and some time before dawn were picked up by armoured cars and taken back to base.

The Edwards' patrol had one unpleasant aftermath. Some days after the incident, a report filtered into Aden that the heads of two English soldiers had been displayed impaled on stakes in the main square of Taiz, across the Yemen border. Ten days later an army patrol reached the area of the SAS position and found two headless bodies buried in a shallow grave. This caused a considerable diplomatic outcry, but the soldiers fighting in the Radfan were not unduly surprised. The soldiery in these tribal areas much resembled a campaign of the old Indian army on the north-west frontier, where quarter is neither given nor expected; a rough region well suited to men of war.

The SAS continued to operate in the Radfan, fighting until the region was abandoned by the British in June 1967. It bridged the gap between their operations in Borneo and a not dissimilar struggle in Oman and Dhufar.

That apart, the late 1960s and 70s was a time when terrorism began to rear its ugly head, not least with the outbreak of the Ulster Troubles in 1968, and counter-terrorism was becoming a major role for the squadrons of the SAS.

12

THE WAR AGAINST THE TERRORIST 1975–92

Adaptability is the key word in the SAS. Adaptability is the key to their success in operations and to the regiment's survival through 30 years of defence reviews, spending cuts, regimental amalgamations and reorganisations. Every decade has offered the regiment a new campaign, a different enemy, fresh terrain to fight in or, as the SAS would see it, another opportunity. The 1970s and 80s were the decades of the terrorist, and all the signs are that terrorism in new forms will continue to plague the world throughout the 90s and beyond.

The statistics of modern terrorism are depressing. In 1969 no fewer than 93 aircraft were hijacked, their crews and passengers tormented, threatened and in some cases killed. Bomb attacks spread throughout the West, with over 100 since 1977 in France, 118 in Germany, 101 in Italy, 60 in Spain and over 50 in Greece. Moreover, terrorist momentum was growing. In Western Europe nearly 2000 people were killed or injured by terrorists in 1983, more than double the figure for 1982. Between 1969 and 1992, over 3000 people were killed in Northern Ireland alone as a result of terrorist activity. Although Palestinian terrorism and that of groups supporting the Palestinian cause seems to be in decline, there is a growing threat from Islamic fundamentalism.

All efforts to stop the terrorist have proved only marginally efficient. Tight airport security did not stop the Lockerbie atrocity when a Boeing 747 airliner was blown out of the sky. Airport security in many parts of the world is still notoriously lax and no deterrent whatsoever to the determined terrorist. The Americans alone now spend over $150 million a year to protect their embassies abroad, with very little effect. The modern terrorist is adaptable, ruthless, often fanatical. With the advantage of surprise, the terrorist can always get through. This being so, the only cure for terrorist activity is a swift and ruthless response.

Terrorism as such is not new. Whether a man, or increasingly, a woman, is a 'terrorist', a 'guerrilla' or a 'freedom fighter', depends on which side you are on. Even going back to Biblical times, a Philistine would probably have felt that King David was a Zionist terrorist. What is new in the 1970s and 80s is the terrorist as an extension of a political faction, often backed by public consensus, guided, trained and paid by governments, inspired by the doctrines of Marx, Hitler or, more recently, Islam. The modern terrorist attacks society directly, preying all too often on innocent bystanders who have no personal involvement in the issues being disputed, displaying ruthlessness toward the victims or hostages, and often publicly supported by outside regimes. Notable exporters of terrorism are Iran, Libya, Bulgaria, Russia and Cuba, but extremist factions or fellow travellers at home are not infrequently their paymasters ('home' in this case being Italy, France, Germany, Japan, the USA or indeed any moderately liberal, democratic society).

By and large, terrorists do not flourish in dictatorships or under despotic regimes. The powers there can be equally ruthless in eliminating opposition, while democratic governments are obliged to be more circumspect, a situation which all too often leads to their political embarrassment, loss of innocent life, and the encouragement of further terrorist acts. Fortunately the democracies are beginning to learn the truth of what the Israelis, who have a long experience of terrorism, have come to call 'The Eleventh Commandment': 'Thou shalt not give in to terrorism.'

In the last ten years most governments have found it necessary to create a counter-revolutionary warfare (CRW) force, often from special force units. Some countries have specially armed and trained police, the so-called SWAT (Special Weapons and Tactics) teams, while some have chosen the military option. The Israelis train small CRW units from their paratroop forces, and used them with great effect to release the captives at Entebbe. The Dutch use marines; the French have an anti-terrorist group from the gendarmerie and elements of the Foreign Legion; the Germans a police detachment, GSG-9; the Americans the Delta Force; the Italians the NOCS; even the Russians have an anti-terrorist unit, the Spetsnaz, formed from their special force units. The British have the SAS.

What these units have in common is a high level of fitness, great skill in close-quarter combat, a supply of specialised weapons and men well trained to use them. Since terrorists are constantly finding fresh targets, these units are constantly developing fresh techniques and, with the (possible) exception of the Russians, usually co-operate in training and sharing operational experience and techniques. The SAS, for example, are trained to enter all makes of passenger aircraft currently in service, working out ways to get in fast and eliminate any opposition. They know how to capture a train, enter a building or regain control of a ship, airport, radio station or oil rig, all likely terrorist targets. Constant training is the only way to ensure that when the call for assistance does come the SAS can act swiftly, effectively and with the minimum loss of life, at least among those hostages or victims who are all too often involved in terrorist incidents.

The SAS entered the war against the terrorist in the early 1970s and almost accidentally, when they offered to provide training in close-quarter combat to the bodyguards protecting foreign heads of state against terrorist attacks, an offer which many governments accepted with alacrity. As a help to this end a curious training aid was constructed at the regimental headquarters in Hereford –

the Close-Quarter Battle (CQB) House, or Killing House. After Western governments appreciated the need to combat terrorism rather than accede to it, counter-terrorism, or, as the SAS call it, counter-revolutionary warfare (CRW) became one of the regiment's prime roles. After the events at the Iranian Embassy in 1980, it was their skill in this role which was to make them world famous.

At this point, as a new phase in the regiment's history opens, and a new role is taken on, it would be as well to look at the modern SAS, both the total regiment and the individual SAS trooper.

It is worth repeating that the 22 SAS Regiment is first and foremost a unit of the British army. The regimental strength is less than that of a line infantry battalion, at about 750 men, and the regiment is organised from top to bottom in units of four. Four men make up a patrol, four patrols a troop, four troops a squadron, four squadrons, each of 72 men and six officers, making up the regiment.

Contrary to the popular belief much fostered by fiction and the media, the SAS soldier is neither a hero nor a superman. He is a self-disciplined, intelligent, highly-trained *specialist*, and the entire object of the much talked about SAS selection and training procedures is designed to find soldiers with the necessary personal qualities and train them for the regiment's particular tasks, while eliminating those who for one reason or another might be more usefully employed elsewhere.

All SAS recruits are drawn from units of the regular army, and will have served about three years with their own corps or regiment before applying for the SAS. This means that the average SAS trooper tends to be older and is probably more mature than the average private soldier found in a line battalion. Generally, NCOs and other ranks join the SAS on an initial three year attachment, which can be renewed for the rest of the man's service, while officers tend to join the SAS for three years and then return to their previous regiments. There are certain exceptions but that is the general picture.

These short attachments have the useful side-effect of

spreading SAS influence throughout the army and eventually gain the regiment friends in all arms and high places. Two well-known British officers, Lt-General Sir Michael Rose and Lt-General de la Billiere, were both formerly SAS officers. General Rose commanded at the Iranian Embassy siege in 1980 and was in charge of United Nations forces in Yugoslavia in 1994. General de la Billiere fought in the Oman and commanded the British forces during the Gulf War.

All SAS candidates drop in rank and pay, and begin by enduring a rigorous selection process at the regimental headquarters in Hereford. Much of this selection and training is carried out in the wild, wet and windy mountains of the Brecon Beacons.

The SAS selection process begins with a ten day fitness and map marching programme which is designed to weed out the basically unfit or unsuitable, a period which terminates with a 40 mile cross-country map march in full kit, carrying platoon weapons, which must be completed in twenty hours or less.

At the end of this process, the number of would-be SAS candidates has fallen dramatically, even if the 'sickener factor', once a feature of SAS training, has now been dropped. The 'sickener factor' was designed to add mental stress to physical effort and, for example, required already tired men to crawl through a deep mud-filled tunnel spiced with rotting sheep's entrails, or having a truck pull up beside them as they marched along and offer a lift – those who even thought of accepting were 'returned to unit'. Or telling them at the apparent end of a shattering march that the actual finish was still three miles away.

Much of this selection activity is carried out alone, or in small groups, for the SAS soldier must display both personal initiative and the ability to work with others. More recently, the training emphasis has changed into encouraging recruits to keep going and complete the course, rather than to put them off, but the basic combination of relentless training and mental stress swiftly weeds out the unfit or the unsuitable.

Those who survive the first phases then go on a fourteen week infantry training course, partly because a surprisingly high proportion of SAS recruits are from corps arms, like the Royal Artillery or Royal Engineers, and not very familiar with basic infantry work, partly to improve basic skills and partly to teach new recruits the use of specific SAS weapons, equipment and techniques, such as sabotage and demolition and, of course, CQB. Then follows the standard army parachute course and training in combat survival, after which the small remnant of the original intake is accepted into the regiment and awarded the much prized beige beret and the 'Who Dares Wins' badge.

Once accepted into the regiment every recruit takes further specialist training. The SAS unit of four system divides every squadron into four specialist troops: the boat troop who are trained as frogmen, in canoeing and small boat handling; the mountain troop trained in climbing, alpine and winter warfare, including skiing; the mobility troop, equipped with machine-gun armed Land Rovers, perhaps the direct descendants of Stirling's jeep-borne warriors of the Western Desert; and the free-fall troop, the high altitude parachutists.

In addition, each troop will contain men with some other particular speciality. There will be a radio man, trained in sending high-speed morse, a medical orderly, trained up to the minor surgery level, and a number of linguists. The SAS believe in speaking the local lingo, whatever it may be, and after Borneo, Aden and the Oman many speak good Arabic or Malay, although nowadays the European languages are becoming popular, notably German and Russian. Finally, all troops are trained in counter-revolutionary warfare (CRW) and take turns by squadron to go on standby at Hereford, ready, if requested, to tackle whatever terrorist emergency might confront the authorities.

Like any other unit of the British army though, the SAS can only operate within Great Britain when requested to do so by the civilian authorities, in a situation described by the military as 'giving aid to the civil power'. A request for such aid must come from the police and would usually require the authority of the Home Secretary. If the regiment accepts the task the matter is then placed in their hands until the situation has been resolved, after which the police will return to centre stage and carry out a full investigation into the incident, ensuring among other things that the SAS have used 'minimum force' to solve the situation and carried out no unnecessary killings. There is no 'licence to kill'.

These are the men and the framework within which they operate. One final consideration is their weaponry. Unlike most other army units, the SAS, and in particular the CRW wing, have virtually a free hand in the choice of weapons. It is likely that any CRW troop will need to work in confined, crowded places, often in the dark, or smoke, and usually in situations of considerable confusion. Their weapons therefore must be short-barrelled, accurate and man-stoppers.

The basic 'entry' equipment of the SAS is the 12-gauge Remington Wingmaster shotgun, a sledgehammer and a pair of bolt-cutters. The Remington's solid shot rounds will blast the hinges off any door, and even if the door is only damaged, a good clout with a 7 lb sledge usually stoves it in. If not, the bolt-cutters will rapidly snip away any chains or interior locks. While this is going on the startled enemy are diverted by magnesium concussion grenades, usually known as 'flash bangs', which will blind and confuse the enemy gunmen for the few vital seconds until the SAS are inside. CS gas can also be employed, which is why the assault team wear gasmasks.

Once the team has entered the terrorist area, be it an embassy or an aircraft, the enemy are eliminated by short bursts from Heckler and Koch MP5 9 mm sub machine-guns. The team will also carry 13-round 9 mm Browning automatics. Given all this equipment, good teamwork and constant training, an SAS counter-revolutionary warfare team can provide a conclusive finale to any terrorist incident. It is fair to say that although they continue to flourish and kill, the palmy days are over for the terrorist. No longer will they be listened to patiently, endured, tolerated and eventually released, flying off to safety in a blaze of TV lights, only to plot fresh crimes. Deep in their mean little souls, the present-day terrorists know that if they push their luck too far, they will be ferried about the world, or held in suspense for the inevitable arrival of the SAS, or some other CRW group. And after that happens, all will be over for yet another group of would-be revolutionary heroes.

The SAS CRW wing had their first taste of the 'real thing' in 1975, at Stansted in Essex, where an Iranian hijacked an airliner with what turned out to be a toy pistol. The SAS arrived, the Iranian wisely surrendered and therefore survived. A few months later, in December 1975, an IRA hit team were surprised in London by officers of the Special Branch and were eventually brought to bay at a small flat in Balcombe Street, where they held two elderly people hostage. The Balcombe Street siege lasted for five days, during which the Metropolitan Police anti-terrorist squad quietly wore down the terrorists' resolve. Then the SAS arrived. Hearing of their arrival on the radio, the IRA terrorists promptly surrendered. So far, no bloodshed. But this happy state of affairs did not characterise the hijacking of a Lufthansa jet which was seized by terrorists in Mallorca and ended up on the runway at Mogadishu in Somalia.

In October 1977, four Palestinian terrorists – two male, two female – joined 79 other holiday passengers on a Lufthansa flight from Mallorca. Security always lapses after a time and baggage checks were obviously minimal, for the terrorists were able to smuggle aboard various weapons and explosives. They then hijacked the aircraft with the objective of forcing the West German Government to free the leaders of the Baader–Meinhof gang, a group of terrorists then imprisoned in Germany. They also demanded a £9 million ransom for the aircraft, passengers and crew. This hijack took place six weeks after the kidnap of a West German industrialist, Hans-Martin

Schleyer, and his release, like that of the Lufthansa hostages, was conditional upon the release of Andreas Baader and Ulrike Meinhof, the terrorist leaders. Schleyer was still a prisoner of the Baader–Meinhof gang when the Lufthansa plane was hijacked. As is usual, these demands were abruptly refused by the German Government and the hijacked jet began to shuttle around the Middle East airports.

While the jet was kept flying about from place to place, a German Government minister travelled to London with a member of the German CRW force, GSG-9, to ask for British help and especially for liaison with the authorities in Dubai where the aircraft was due to land. The Bonn Government wanted the British to arrange diplomatic clearance for GSG-9 to attack the aircraft at Dubai, while the GSG-9 representative believed that his SAS opposite number in Britain might supply certain equipment which would be most useful for entering the aircraft. The SAS had actually trained the soldiers of the Dubai Presidential Guard, and it soon became apparent that SAS assistance would be extremely helpful. The two SAS men chosen to assist GSG-9 were Major Alastair Morrison and Sergeant Barry Davies. After collecting a supply of 'flash bangs' from Hereford, they left for Dubai.

There they found that the GSG-9's team leader and two of his men were firmly under Dubai police guard in the airport's VIP lounge, while the hijacked aircraft with its hostages stood on the melting tarmac of the ramp outside. Morrison and Davies swiftly cut through the red tape and briefed the Dubai Royal Guard in CRW techniques, with the idea that they would provide a back-up force for GSG-9, whose main force was due to arrive shortly. However, before any attack could be carried out the Lufthansa aircraft with its hostages still aboard took off and flew to Aden, soon followed by another aircraft carrying Morrison, Davies, Wegener (GSG-9's team leader) and the other two GSG-9 men.

The Aden Government refused the GSG-9 team permission to land, so they flew on to Mogadishu in Somalia, where they were joined by the rest of their force. Here the group drew up their plans to assault the aircraft at the earliest opportunity. The SAS men were to break down the emergency doors and hurl the 'flash bang' grenades at the commencement of the operation, after which the GSG-9 men would enter the aircraft and finish the job. The Germans really wanted a less risky outcome and the GSG-9 team actually carried the £9 million ransom money with them.

In Aden, events took a dramatic turn for the worse when the Lufthansa captain was murdered by the terrorist leader in full sight of the passengers. This was too much for the Aden authorities, who ordered the aircraft to leave. At the orders of the terrorist leader, the aircraft took off and the second pilot flew it . . . to Mogadishu. Here, the captain's body was thrown from the aircraft onto the tarmac, having lain on the aircraft's floor throughout the flight, in full view of the frightened hostages.

At the sight of the body on the runway, all hopes of a peaceful end to the affair were abandoned and that night the CRW forces went into action. The SAS men blew in the emergency exit doors above the wings on each side of the fuselage and the GSG-9 men burst in. Inside they had to gun down terrorists positioned at the front and rear of the plane. Petrol and alcohol from the duty free bar had been splashed over the passengers and the interior of the plane, and could well have exploded into flames. Fortunately this didn't happen, although the terrorists hurled a couple of hand grenades at the assault team, which exploded harmlessly under empty seats. The hostages were strapped in their seats and kept below the line of fire, which, in the space of eight minutes, killed three terrorists. The leader proved to be a professional gunman working for the Palestinians but operating on behalf of the West German Baader–Meinhof group. None of the passengers were injured.

Then, in the spring of 1980, came the most famous incident in the SAS's long and lively history: the Iranian Embassy siege. The Iranian Embassy siege in London, which ended so dramatically before the television cameras on 6 May 1980, had been going on for six days before the SAS moved in.

The embassy staff, all followers of the Iranian fundamentalist leader, Ayatollah Khomeini, had been seized by six anti-Khomeini terrorists. The terrorists had also gathered up the British policeman guarding the embassy door, PC Trevor Lock, and a BBC man, Sim Harris, who was conducting an interview at the embassy when the terrorists broke in. The terrorists wanted the Iranian Government to offer autonomy to one of the Iranian regions, and threatened to kill members of the staff until this demand was met.

The British Government and the police, who were initially involved in the siege, found the whole affair complicated by three novel factors: the belief of the Iranian Government that Britain had inspired the terrorists, the presence in the streets around the embassy of a mob of chanting, praying, pro-Khomeini supporters and an ever-growing crowd of reporters and TV crews. This siege of the Iranian Embassy in London, coming so soon after the long agony of the American Embassy affair in Tehran, when the Iranians held the American staff hostage for many months, caught the imagination of the world.

The SAS at Hereford were alerted as soon as the siege began, and the matter was passed into the hands of the duty CRW team. When the embassy press attaché was shot dead and his body dumped on the doorstep with the declaration that the terrorists would shoot a hostage every 45 minutes until their demands were met, the SAS went into action.

Inside the embassy there were a total of twenty hostages, and by now their positions had been located. There were fifteen men in Room 10, overlooking the street. The terrorists had moved them there a few hours previously, believing that there would soon be an asssault by the security forces. This group was guarded by three of the terrorists, who periodically took it in turns to move around the building checking the other rooms. In Room

9, five women hostages were guarded by one terrorist. The position of the remaining two terrorists varied. The only means of entry was at the front, through a window on the first floor balcony, glazed with armour plate glass which would have to be blown in.

It is some indication of how carefully the assault had been pre-planned that the SAS went in within eleven minutes of the time the body of the press attaché was dumped on the embassy steps. Their arrival was both swift and dramatic.

Black-clad men appeared on the rooftop balconies, swung down on ropes and placed charges of plastic explosive against the bullet-proof glass of the first-floor front window, while four pairs of SAS men reached the roof to begin their descent on ropes down the back wall of the embassy. The first abseiling party started to descend at the rear, but one of them swung into an upper storey window, hitting the window with his boot and smashing the glass. The terrorist leader, hearing the sound of breaking glass, went to investigate, followed by PC Lock, who was still in his full uniform, complete with overcoat, under which he had managed to keep concealed his .38 inch revolver. The first SAS pair dropped to the ground at the back of the building and prepared to shoot their way into it, while the second abseil team was already on the rear first-floor balcony, breaking the window and throwing in the first of several 'flash bang' grenades. Another team started down the rope, but one man became trapped on the abseil rope and was unable to move. His comrades couldn't now fire their charges without risk to him, so they smashed in the ground floor windows and swarmed in, while the SAS team on the first floor were shooting it out with the terrorist leader, who had been tackled by PC Lock. Lock managed to draw his pistol, but the terrorist had struggled free and was about to open fire when the SAS shot him down.

Much of this action took place in front of television cameras ranged just across the road. Before millions of transfixed TV viewers, two more SAS soldiers blew in the bullet-proof front window. An enormous explosion destroyed the heavy glass and the SAS stormed into the room through the smoke and dashed up the stairs. Outside, other members of the team fired a CS gas cartridge into a room near the top of the embassy where the last terrorist was believed to be hiding. The curtains burst into flames and very soon fire broke out and swept through the room, scorching the SAS soldier from the third rear team, who was still trapped outside on his abseil rope. His comrades cut the rope to let him drop to a balcony, whereupon he picked himself up and joined the rest of the team in the embassy building, coming face to face with an armed terrorist whom he shot dead.

As soon as the firing began, the terrorist guards in Room 10 at the front of the building, started to shoot their hostages and had killed the assistant press attaché, and wounded the chargé d'affaires before the SAS broke in. Another hostage only escaped injury when a bullet was deflected by a 50p coin in his pocket. The terrorists then tried to pretend that they, too, were hostages, but were quickly identified and shot, while the last terrorist was located and killed in a room on the top floor. The only terrorist to escape death was the one guarding the women in Room 9. The women refused to identify him as a terrorist and he was finally captured and handed over quietly to the police after the shooting was over. By now the upper floors of the embassy were well alight, and so in a cloud of smoke and a blaze of glory, the SAS quietly faded away.

The embassy affair gave the SAS a great deal of somewhat unwelcome publicity, but it did at least teach would-be terrorists a lesson: that the patience of the British Government is not inexhaustible. If terrorism is still uncommon on the streets of Britain, some thanks must go to the speedy action and skill demonstrated to the world by that CRW team of the SAS.

No account of the SAS can close without some reference to the regiment's role in Northern Ireland. Some believe that the SAS were involved there from the start, but their presence on the border was finally admitted in 1974, six years after the troubles began. Few official details of their activities since have been issued to the Press, but the SAS have certainly clashed frequently with the IRA and given a very good account of themselves, notably in the so-called bandit country of South Armagh. But before the regiment could extend their role in Northern Ireland they were called away to the South Atlantic to fight in the Falklands War of 1982.

13

THE SAS IN THE FALKLANDS 1982

If adaptability is one watchword for the SAS, action is another. The SAS like to get involved in any conflict and are never backward in coming forward to offer their services if there is a chance of action. As soon as the CO of 22 SAS heard of the Argentine landings in the Falkland Islands on 2 April 1982, he put the regiment on standby and phoned Brigadier Julian Thompson, who was commanding 3 Commando Brigade, Royal Marines at Stonehouse Barracks in Plymouth.

If the British were to retake the Falklands, then it was certain that the commando brigade, the one British unit fully trained in amphibious warfare, would lead the assault, and when the British went ashore, the SAS intended to be there. SAS soldiers were summoned back from all parts of the world, from training teams in the Middle East, from patrols in the 'bandit country' of South Armagh, from scattered semi-secret operations, to take part at last on a real, big war, one which would employ ships and aircraft and artillery and offer good scope for the raiding and reconnaissance skills of the SAS.

Task force operations to retake the Falkland Islands began with the recapture of Grytviken, the port in South Georgia, a task executed by D Squadron 22 SAS, the Royal Marine detachment from the destroyer HMS *Antrim*, part of M Company, 42 Commando, Royal Marines, and 2 Special Boat Section Royal Marines, making a total force of about 75 well-assorted fighting men.

On the night this force went ashore, the Argentine submarine *Santa Fé* was tied up in Grytviken harbour, unloading reinforcements for the Argentine garrison and was due to sail at dawn on the 25 April. Lieutenant Commander Stanley, flying a Wessex helicopter, was on his way back to HMS *Antrim* after dropping the SBS men a few miles from Grytviken when he observed a submarine on the surface, which he promptly attacked and straddled with depth charges, causing sufficient damage to the pressure hull to make it unwise for the submarine to dive. Listing badly and leaking oil, the submarine limped towards the safety of Grytviken and was attacked yet again on the way by helicopters from HMS *Endurance* and the frigate *Brilliant*. These attacks killed several of the crew and riddled the conning tower with cannon fire.

The unexpected return of the submarine in sinking condition caused a near panic among the Argentine garrison ashore. Machine-gun emplacements fired at the circling helicopters as the submarine crew dashed for cover, and the D Squadron commander and Guy Sheridan of the Royal Marines decided to use this diversion to move in and take the port. The garrison outnumbered the attacking force by two to one, but the Argentines seemed demoralised and were not making any effective defence moves.

Supported by gunfire from HMS *Antrim* and *Plymouth*, the landing force prepared to go ashore. The SAS were landed by helicopter from HMS *Plymouth*, followed by Royal Marines of 42 Commando with mortars and a naval gunfire support officer to direct the guns from the ships. Shells fell all around the Argentine positions and added to the already considerable state of alarm.

Once ashore, sheltered from Grytviken by a small hill, the landing force struck out and began to advance on the port, clearing enemy positions as they went and calling down naval gunfire support by radio when held up by a machine-gun post.

From Brown Mountain ridge the British troops had a clear view of Grytviken harbour, including the oil-smeared conning tower of the sunken *Sante Fé* submarine. Every building in the town was decorated with white sheets and the garrison surrendered without a shot, although the assault party were lucky to escape injury when they walked unawares through a minefield. British forces were once again ashore in South Georgia. A few days later, the SAS went ashore in the Falkland Islands proper, to attack Argentine aircraft at the airstrip on Pebble Island.

Pebble Island lies off the northern coast of West Falkland, one of the two large islands in the Falkland group. In early May 1982 it was garrisoned by a small force from an Argentine infantry regiment, protecting a troop of engineers who were preparing an airstrip for the use of Argentine Pucara ground attack fighters and constructing a radar station. This base, once operational, would not only present the task force with an increased danger of attack from the highly effective Pucaras, but the radar would also give the Argentine commanders excellent information on the movements of the British fleet. The task of eliminating the Argentines on the Pebble Island base was entrusted to the boat troop and mountain troop of D Squadron, 22 SAS. Operations began with a recce of the target.

The route planned for the raid involved transportation by helicopter to a remote promontory, Mare's Rock on West Falkland. From there they would round the peninsula in canoes and, having established that the enemy coast was clear, paddle across under cover of darkness to land on Pebble Island. From the beach it was about ten miles to the airstrip and this distance would have to be covered on foot.

When put into effect this plan at once ran into difficulty, the first obstacle being that the thundering surf made it quite impossible for them to launch their collapsible Klepper canoes. Boat troop therefore climbed back into the helicopter, which was recalled by radio, and flew in towards their observation post on the north of West Falkland. Here they set up an OP (observation post) and kept close watch on Pebble Island. As it grew dark they launched their canoes and all arrived safely on Pebble Island several hours before midnight.

One patrol established a beachhead here with a radio link back to HMS *Hermes*, while the second four-man patrol moved on through the night towards their objective, where they lay up till daylight. At dawn they saw that there were eleven Argentine aircraft on the strip, about 2000 metres away from the patrol's hiding place, but between the patrol and their targets the ground was flat and totally devoid of cover. Sentries were plentiful, but the recce patrol had seen all they needed to see. Abandoning their rucksacks they crawled away into dead ground and laid up there throughout the rest of the day, marching hurriedly back to the beachhead at night to signal the information to HMS *Hermes*.

The original plan for the raid envisaged the SAS wiping out the garrison and destroying all the aircraft, but there was not sufficient time or helicopters available to put this into effect, and with every hour that passed the SAS recce group on the beachhead stood the risk of detection. The aircraft were the first priority and so the attack was scaled down and the recce group were joined that night by twenty men from mountain troop, flown into the beachhead in three helicopters from HMS *Hermes*.

Put like that it sounds simple, but it is as well to remember that this operation was carried out at night, without lights, into enemy-held territory, and at wave-hopping height. Fortunately the moon came to light up the cold, clear night after the raiders were ashore, and the approach to the airfield was completed swiftly. Just before dawn, at 0700 hours, the raiders were in position.

The attack began with an impressive display of firepower from small arms and rockets, which destroyed several Argentine aircraft. The resulting confusion was kept going by the guns of HMS *Glamorgan*, which poured shells on the Argentine infantry positions. With the enemy heads well down, the SAS now strode onto the airstrip and set about blowing up any remaining aircraft and all the ammunition, petrol and stores they could find. One man was injured by shrapnel, but by 0715 the airfield was ablaze and the troops began to withdraw. By 0930 hours, on time to the second, naval helicopters swept in to lift the SAS away. Thus ended a textbook SAS operation against considerable, if ineffective, odds.

The Falklands campaign added fresh leaves to SAS laurels, but as always, these laurels are not gained without loss. A few days after their successful attack on Pebble Island, men of the regiment were being transferred by night from the carrier HMS *Hermes* to the assault ship HMS *Intrepid*, in preparation for another operation. Somewhere between the two ships, something small, probably a seagull, was sucked into the main engine of the Sea King helicopter, which fell at once into the sea. Although a search began at once, no one could survive for long in the icy waters of the South Atlantic. In all the SAS and their various supporting specialists lost twenty men in this one incident, the regiment's largest single loss since the Second World War.

The regiment was shocked but not discouraged by these casualties, even though all those lost were old friends and many of them vital elements in the regimental hierarchy. The SAS fought on throughout the campaign, at Goose Green, in San Carlos Water, on Mount Kent, and on the final advance into Stanley. When the campaign was over they came home again, but quietly, slipping back to Hereford, avoiding the crowds and the cameras, ready for a spot of leave and then their return to whatever new tasks and fresh enemies fortune put in their way. The SAS squadrons dispersed to various tasks, but their main role for the rest of the decade would take place amid the lanes and dank streets of Northern Ireland, in a bitter fight against the IRA.

14

THE SAS IN NORTHERN IRELAND

Although there are now some hopes that the problems in Northern Ireland are at last on the point of being resolved, the current round of 'troubles' in Ireland has been going on for more than a quarter of a century. In that time they have cost more than 3000 lives and resulted in the destruction of billions of pounds worth of property for no valid reason or perceptible advantage. The personal and financial costs of this tragedy are only a part of it.

The 26-year campaign in Ireland has actually been a very nasty little war. It has been fought with a great deal of bloodshed and a legacy of hatred between the Catholic and Protestant communities, between the Republicans and Unionists, that no amount of political manoeuvring will really wish away. It sprang from nearly 400 years of conflict between the two communities and only a real optimist could say with confidence that the 'troubles' are finally over.

Although there has never been any possibility of a military solution to the Ulster problem, at least without a prior political settlement, the British army has been closely involved with the province since troops were first committed there in 1969, some months after a series of civil rights marches were brutally broken up by elements of the Royal Ulster Constabulary.

Those soldiers who went to Belfast and other Northern Ireland towns in 1969 recall that they were welcomed with open arms by the local population, Catholic and

Protestant, invited into their homes and plied with plates of sandwiches and cups of tea. This friendliness did not last.

There was renewed sectarian fighting, the troops who moved in to stop it were attacked by mobs from both sides, the IRA moved into the Catholic housing estates and the long bloody all too familiar Northern Ireland conflict began and dragged on for decades. Although the number has varied from time to time, there are usually about 15,000 British soldiers deployed in Ulster, in an 'Aid to the Civil Power' role. Among this number are the men of the 22nd Special Air Service Regiment.

The regiment were first deployed in Northern Ireland in August 1969, quite openly, in uniform and in squadron strength. D Squadron were based at the Bessbrook camp in South Armagh – in what came to be known as bandit country – and one of the squadron's first actions was to hold a formal parade and wreath-laying at the grave of Lt-Col Blair 'Paddy' Mayne, who had been killed in a motor accident after the war and now lies in the cemetery at Newtownards.

That apart, the squadron took part in routine patrol duties and road blocks, still in uniform and wearing their own sand-coloured SAS berets. Matters were still relatively peaceful so the SAS squadron was eventually withdrawn and sent to join the rest of the regiment in the Oman. The SAS returned to Northern Ireland in 1974 and have remained there ever since, apart from short deployments to Arabia during the Gulf War.

The situation in Northern Ireland had deteriorated considerably in the intervening years, especially along the border and in South Armagh, which has a strongly Nationalist population, much of it concentrated in the town of Crossmaglen. The SAS returned to Bessbrook camp and began to work in conjunction with the resident battalion. At this time the SAS began to go under cover.

At first the disguise was minimal. When 40 Commando, Royal Marines were at Bessbrook, the SAS put on green berets; when the Parachute Regiment arrived, the

SAS went over to red berets; and when a Highland battalion appeared in South Armagh, the SAS went about in bonnets. Before long however, the SAS were operating in civilian clothes, in private cars and on both sides of the border.

Soldiering in civilian clothes became quite common in Northern Ireland. It was highly inadvisable for a soldier to go about on his own at all, and definitely dangerous to be alone and in uniform. Some other units also took on patrolling South Armagh in plain clothes, even equipping the outside of their car with anti-personnel 'claymore' mines which could be detonated with lethal effect if the soldiers ran into one of the VCPs (vehicle check or control points) which the Provisional IRA (PIRA) had got into the habit of setting up on the roads around Crossmaglen.

In Ulster, as in other such situations, the prime requirement in the fight against terrorism is sound intelligence. Before long Ulster was awash with intelligence units and operatives – so many that they got in each other's way. The prime source should have been the Royal Ulster Constabulary and their Special Branch but this force had made itself so unpopular with the Catholic community that it could find very few informers and therefore produced very little usable information.

Other agencies then arrived to take a hand in the game. MI5 came to oversee matters in Northern Ireland and MI6 began to track PIRA personnel in the Republic. The army, drawing on its experience in Malaya, Kenya and elsewhere, did succeed in finding a number of informers – 'touts' to the PIRA people – and a number of former IRA who for cash or from conviction were willing to work against their former comrades. Known as 'Freds', though designated the Military Reconnaissance Force, any Fred captured by PIRA faced a grisly fate of torture and a bullet in the head. The RUC strengthened their Special Branch and introduced armed roving Special Patrol Group units.

Another element in this complicated brew was the 14th Intelligence Company, a group of police and army volunteers who worked in plain clothes and were raised in 1974 by Lt-Col Frank Kitson, who was an acknowledged expert in covert or low intensity warfare. This profusion of intelligence gathering did not greatly improve either the quantity or quality of the intelligence brought in.

The plain fact was that no one was happy with the state of intelligence gathering but rather than improve the Special Branch of the Royal Ulster Constabulary, the body that ought to have had eyes and ears everywhere in Northern Ireland, each element in the brew set up their own intelligence gathering unit, which led to unhealthy competition and a diffusion of effort.

Intelligence gathering is one of the principal roles of the SAS, which gathers intelligence in the main by surveillance rather than by running informers. SAS patrols would set up surveillance patrols at crossing points on the border, on the houses of men known to be active in the IRA – 'known players' in the jargon of the time – and on the paths, tracks and country roads surrounding Crossmaglen and other IRA strongholds. This is boring, cold, damp work but in the end it produces results.

The regiment had been at this task for some time before the British Government announced in January 1976 that elements of the SAS had indeed been deployed in the province for patrolling and surveillance duties.

This deployment was quite different from the first commitment in 1969. Only a dozen troopers were involved, and they worked as described above with the regular battalions already on the ground. Within a few weeks, and certainly by the spring of 1976 there was a full SAS squadron at Bessbrook, sending four-man patrols out by day and night to quarter the countryside of South Armagh. Results were not long in coming.

On the night of 12 March a drunken Irishman wandering about just north of the border was picked up by an army patrol. The soldiers took him in and ran his details through the police computer and found they had caught a major 'player', Sean McKenna.

Mr McKenna was most unhappy about his arrest, claiming that he had been asleep in bed in his house south of the border when three masked men had entered the room, dragged him off into South Armagh and handed him over, shocked but stone-cold sober, to the soldiers. Mr McKenna was tried for a long list of crimes and sent to prison for 25 years and his capture was credited to a snatch operation by the SAS. The Irish Government was none too happy about British soldiers crossing their frontier, but nothing much was said officially at the time.

In April 1976 the SAS notched up their first kill. After a tip-off that Patrick Cleary, a noted IRA 'player', was about to cross the border to see his girlfriend, the SAS ambushed the girl's house and when Cleary arrived he was promptly arrested. What happened after that is obscure but the inquest decided that Cleary had attempted to escape and been shot down while doing so. Sinn Fein and the IRA claimed that Cleary had been murdered.

Then matters went embarrassingly awry. On the evening of 5 May 1976, the gardai – the Irish police – stopped a car with Irish plates a few hundred yards south of the border. The men inside were armed and a few moments later, as more gardai arrived, so did two more cars from north of the border. The drivers and passengers of these cars were also armed but made no resistance when the gardai arrested them. It then transpired that the gardai had picked up eight SAS soldiers, south of the border in plain clothes and heavily armed. The publicity was considerable, and very unfavourable to the British Army. The IRA were delighted.

The Irish Government played the matter well. They clearly could not tolerate such incursions but the eight men, having been bailed, were subsequently fined £100 each and released. The matter however was not closed. The Ulster–Ireland border is wide open and although many of the minor roads had been blocked or cratered, the local people tended to fill in the craters and remove the barricades.

British soldiers had to be very careful to avoid trespassing into the Republic but the IRA had a safe haven where the British army could not pursue them. The gardai would follow up on leads provided from north of the border but by the time they arrived the IRA gunmen had usually disappeared. The only real chance to strike at the IRA was to catch them in the act.

An SAS patrol did just that in January 1977 when they elected to mount surveillance on a parked car close to Crossmaglen. A few nights later a masked and armed man was seen approaching the car and when challenged by the hidden SAS men he raised his weapon and was promptly shot down. There was then some supporting fire from more IRA men further down the road and a heavy exchange of fire before the IRA fled.

The deadly nature of this border war was bloodily underlined again in May 1977 when an IRA unit operating from a base in the Republic entered Armagh and kidnapped a guards officer, Captain Robert Nairac. Captain Nairac was serving in the 14th Intelligence Company and had elected to visit a bar in South Armagh, alone and in plain clothes, though armed with an automatic pistol. He was attacked in the car-park outside the pub, bundled into a car and taken across the border where he was tortured and killed.

During 1977 SAS strength in Ulster rose to a full squadron, and the three troops were deployed at various brigade headquarters around the province, with the fourth troop in reserve under the command of the Commander Land Forces, Northern Ireland. Then came two incidents which brought the whole issue of SAS involvement into question. In June 1978 three IRA men were caught in an SAS ambush and killed while attempting to plant a bomb in a post office at Ballyskillen.

A fourth IRA man ran off from the car and escaped, but in the pursuit the SAS – or the RUC Special Patrol Group who were also involved – also killed a Mr William Hanna who was simply returning home from a pub. The army press office put out a statement saying that the IRA had opened fire first and that Mr Hanna had been killed in the crossfire.

It then came out that the three IRA men, though clearly

on a terrorist mission, had been unarmed, so there could be no question of any 'crossfire'. It eventually transpired that Mr Hanna had simply been shot down by mistake. The damage to the reputation of the SAS and the British army caused by this tragic accident was nothing compared with the criticism raised by the attempted cover up.

Worse was to follow just a month later. In July 1977 a farmer's son, John Boyle, discovered a cache of IRA weapons in a cemetery at Dunloy in County Antrim. His father rang the police and a four-man SAS patrol took up position overlooking the cache, ready to ambush those who came to lift it. Unfortunately, no one thought to tell the Boyle family of this ambush or order them to stay away.

As a result, the 16-year-old John Boyle decided to see if the weapons were still there and went back for a look. When he picked up one of the weapons for a closer inspection, two hidden SAS marksmen shot him dead. His father and brother, who came running up to investigate, were rather more lucky; they were leapt on, forced to the ground and taken off to the police station in a helicopter; only then was the full extent of the tragedy discovered.

Once again the army attempted to wriggle out of the situation by telling a pack of lies. The first claim was that John Boyle had pointed a loaded weapon at the patrol; John Boyle had no idea that the patrol was even there and he had no knowledge of firearms. The next claim was that a warning had been shouted to him and ignored. This lie was also soon refuted. The RUC responded to growing public concern by arresting two SAS men who were subsequently put on trial for murder.

They were eventually acquitted because the prosecution failed to make their case – that the men intended to shoot and kill anyone who approached the cache. It did transpire however that the RUC had remembered to warn the Boyles to stay away from the cemetery – but the call had not been made until the family had left for their fields.

These incidents put the SAS in a bad light. Soldiers serving in Northern Ireland – or anywhere else – are bound by a set of instructions generally referred to as the Rules of Engagement. In the delicate situation in Northern Ireland these rules are set out plainly on a yellow card, which every soldier has to carry, know by heart and apply. The SAS are also soldiers in the British army and bound by yellow card rules.

The essence of the yellow card rules is an insistence on minimum force. The troops are not to open fire unless first fired at or unless they think beyond all possible – or reasonable – doubt that their lives or those of their friends are in danger. A warning should also be given before opening fire. These yellow card rules, if applied to the letter, would make safe soldiering impossible, but they are designed to protect innocent citizens and bystanders against wild shooting and irresponsible gunplay.

Even so, rules that seem sensible and easy to apply in a warm barrack room take on quite a different meaning when a car is roaring through an ambush position, or a man looms up out of the night carrying what appears to be a weapon. He who hesitates at such a moment could easily end up dead.

Clearly, therefore, yellow card rules have to be applied with reference to the situation and the same criteria should apply to any subsequent enquiry. However, there were grounds for serious disquiet. The fact that two innocent unarmed men had now been shot dead and a further three far-from-innocent but still unarmed IRA men had also been killed, all without the benefit of a warning, was too much to allow for. The lies churned out by the army press offices did nothing to make the situation any better. It would have been far better to admit the mistake, explain the situation at the time, apologise and offer compensation; instead the army attempted to place the blame on the victims, who were dead and in no position to argue.

These tragic accidents were to continue. In September 1977 Mr James Taylor was out with a shotgun for some rough shooting when he stumbled on an SAS patrol who shot him dead. Mr Taylor was a Protestant with no connections with any paramilitary group, and this time the army told the truth and apologised. In the following November an SAS team infiltrated a house in Londonderry where another IRA cache of arms had been located. A known player, Patrick Duffy, entered the house and went to the cache only to be challenged and shot dead by the soldiers. Mr Duffy was not armed and questions were inevitably raised about why the four soldiers in the house did not simply arrest him.

Following this affair the SAS were withdrawn from ambush duties and returned to a more conventional surveillance role. This role was not without risk and in May 1980 the regiment suffered its first death in Northern Ireland when Captain Herbert Westacott, commanding one of the troops in G Squadron was shot dead while commanding a party cordoning off a house in Belfast. Later that year a team of SAS scored a *coup* when they surrounded a farmhouse in Fermanagh and caught four IRA men including a very notorious player, Seamus McElwaine. On this occasion, a warning was given, and the IRA thought it over and elected to surrender.

During most of 1982 the SAS were engaged in the Falklands War and maintained only a small presence in Northern Ireland but after Port Stanley fell, the SAS made their way back into the province. In December 1982 the SAS killed two armed IRA men after a two-day stake out of a weapons cache near Coalisland while in July 1983 two teams scored a major success after a tip-off about a forthcoming IRA attack in County Tyrone.

Ths IRA intended to bomb a factory making kitchen equipment and, hearing of this plan, the SAS set up an ambush and prepared to wait. They did not have to wait long. Soon after dark, two men were seen approaching, and were challenged and fired upon when they failed to halt. One man was wounded and both were captured. Then two more IRA men were discovered and fired upon and this time one was captured and one killed. Two men were later imprisoned for this attempted outrage.

The next IRA–SAS encounter had a far less happy outcome. Attempting to thwart the murder of a member of the Ulster Defence Regiment, the SAS set up an ambush. The IRA killers duly arrived and were fired upon but the only person killed was a civilian, Fred Jackson. Mr Jackson was calling on a timber yard just across the road from the ambush site when the soldiers opened fire. A bullet hit him in the chest and he died instantly.

In December 1984 a second SAS man was killed in the province during the course of a successful attempt to prevent an IRA active service unit planting a churn bomb under a road. Four IRA men in a van were stopped by three SAS men; as two of the SAS approached the van, they were fired on by IRA men hidden in the hedges and Lance-Corporal Slater was killed. In the fight that followed two IRA men died. One was shot in the action, and another drowned while attempting to swim a river and get back to the safety of the Republic where the two surviving PIRA men were arrested by the police.

The SAS and the IRA clearly had their teeth set into each other and a further incident was not long in coming. Again the IRA were attempting to murder a member of the Ulster Defence Regiment. This is a volunteer part-time force and the target soldier usually worked as an orderly in a hospital in Derry. This intention was leaked to the police and a team of soldiers moved into the hospital to await events.

The murder was entrusted to two experienced killers, Daniel Doherty and William Fleming, who entered the hospital grounds on a motorbike. According to evidence given at the subsequent inquest, the pair rode past a car containing SAS men and the pillion passenger was seen to be holding a pistol. The car driver therefore chased and rammed the motorcycle, and both men were thrown off. Fleming, the passenger, was fired on by two SAS men, hit six times and killed. Doherty remounted the machine and attempted to escape but he too was shot and killed.

In February 1985 there was another fatal encounter when a roving group of five IRA killers, driving around seeking someone to kill near Strabane, roamed into an SAS ambush and three were killed. A fourth man was captured later and the last one fled. Following this shooting tales got about that the three men had been murdered. It appeared that all three had received a bullet in the back of the head and some local people claimed that at least one voice had been heard calling for mercy before the final burst of fire. The inquest failed to find any evidence to support this last claim and a verdict of 'lawful killing' was brought in.

The shooting at Strabane ushered in a quiet couple of years but there were some further incidents. In February 1986 a cache was located in Londonderry and placed under surveillance. A man called Francis Bradley later entered the yard, was challenged by an SAS soldier and shot dead when he turned in response to the call. This caused further disquiet for not only did Mr Bradley have no terrorist connections, but he was unarmed, had reacted normally to the challenge and had been shot no less than eight times.

So it went on. It would be wrong to think that the SAS role in Northern Ireland involved a constant round of ambush and excitement. Many soldiers served for years in Northern Ireland without firing a shot or hearing an explosion. The old tale, that soldiering is 'long periods of intense boredom interspersed with short periods of intense terror' is true of all wars, not just those in Ireland.

If the SAS saw more than their fair share of excitement, that went with their role as the cutting edge for a number of intelligence units. The intelligence people found the leads and contacts and the SAS went in to do the shooting. Even so, it took a great deal of work to make a contact and at best the SAS were only making one every two or three months, with plenty of months passing without any action at all, though the IRA and other paramilitary units continued to murder and kneecap their victims on an almost daily basis.

In April 1987 the IRA killed an elderly English judge and his wife who lived in Ireland and were returning home after a holiday in England. A month later however, the IRA got a considerable drubbing in the village of Loughgall in North Armagh.

The IRA intended to bomb a small police station using a massive bomb mounted in the bucket of a JCB excavator. The importance of good intelligence has been made over and over again in this book and here again it was this that tipped off the RUC about the forthcoming attack. This information, which turned out to be highly accurate, was passed on to the SAS who were in position, in and around the police station, before the IRA appeared.

Early in the evening of Friday 8 May, a Toyota van rolled into the village followed by the JCB with three armed IRA men riding on it. Three men jumped out of the van and opened fire on the police station as the JCB rammed the perimeter fence.

This attack was met with a storm of fire from the hidden SAS men, which killed the three men riding on the JCB and the driver of the van. A great blast of explosive then almost demolished the police station and the JCB. Two more men were found dead inside the van and another man was killed as he attempted to shelter under it. The IRA had lost a good many key players and the SAS had scored a notable victory . . . and then it went wrong.

Just before the attack two brothers, Oliver and Anthony Hughes, drove into the village, where all seemed quiet. The men were mechanics and were wearing their blue overalls, which were similar to the dress worn by the IRA for the attack. When the firing started the two men decided to reverse up the road but on the way the soldiers opened fire on their truck, killing Anthony and severely wounding Oliver. No challenge was given because the action had already commenced.

In November 1987 came the senseless and brutal IRA attack during the Remembrance Day Service in the centre of Enniskillen, when a bomb hidden in the war memorial went off, killing eleven people and injuring a great many more. The pattern of killing has continued up to the end of 1994 when a ceasefire was announced by PIRA, pending talks about the future of Northern Ireland.

It may hold and it might work. After 26 years of killing and sectarian violence it can only be hoped that reason has finally prevailed though it is hard to see what process of reconciliation can lead to a settlement that both Republicans and Unionists will be willing to accept.

As far as the army and the SAS in particular are concerned, Northern Ireland has been a mixed blessing. Patrolling with a bullet up the spout and learning to soldier when your life is at risk, however remote that risk might be, is a good way to give an army that extra little edge. That edge gave the British a clear advantage in the South Atlantic but the lessons of Northern Ireland are not all good ones. Actions in aid of the civil power should only be entered into when all else has failed and carry the risk that soldiers will become involved in actions for which their training and temperament has left them less than well equipped.

No army in the world has displayed – or could display – the good humour, courage and long-suffering conduct of the soldiers of the British army. Most of them are quite young and of junior rank, and often subjected to long and severe provocation. The question that has to be asked is: should the troops be placed in this position at all? One lesson that might come out of the Northern Ireland business is that soldiers should only be committed to such a task in certain circumstances and as a last resort – a lesson underlined most clearly by what happened on the Rock of Gibraltar in March 1988.

15

DEATH IN GIBRALTAR

The full extent of the undercover anti-terrorist work conducted by the SAS in Northern Ireland has never been wholly disclosed but it is certain that the regiment took a leading role both in reconnaissance duties in South Armagh and along the border and in ambushes of IRA active service units caught *en route* to some terrorist action. The IRA have always known that terrorism on the British mainland or in continental Europe was less risky and of a higher publicity value than a strike against a target in Ulster and in March 1988 the IRA extended their range to the Rock of Gibraltar.

The 'Death on the Rock' affair, as it came to be called, led to the death of three IRA terrorists – Sean Savage, Daniel McCann and a woman, Maraid Farrell, each with a long record of terrorist activity. The story is complicated and controversial so it would be as well to take it one step at a time. British Intelligence, especially MI5, had long maintained a close watch on known terrorists and terrorist sympathisers and in the autumn of 1987 located two known players, Savage and McCann, touring along the Costa del Sol. The pair stayed in the area, or made frequent visits throughout the winter of 1987–8, and since the most obvious target was the British garrison of Gibraltar, a close-surveillance team from MI5 flew out there in early 1988 and drew up a list of possible targets.

The most obvious of these was a car bomb attack on one of the regular ceremonial events – the changing of the guard at the Governor's Palace for which a military band and troops paraded through the streets. Military ceremonies and military bands had provided the IRA with several bloody opportunities in recent years and all the signs were that another such bloodbath was being planned for Gibraltar. It was known that the IRA had developed a remote-control, hand-held triggering device which could probably detonate a car bomb from a safe distance. Maraid Farrell arrived in Malaga on 4 March 1988 and joined up with Savage and McCann so it seemed likely that the attack was about to take place quite soon. The first task of the security services was to work out the time and place of the attack and if possible find and neutralise the bomb. The Spanish police were aware of the situation and willing to co-operate in the search for the car bomb and a sixteen-man team from the SAS, in plain clothes, was flown to Gibraltar on 3 March to work with the police on the Rock. A full-scale security operation was now in hand and given the code name of FLAVIUS.

Anti-terrorist operations are conducted by the army when requested, under the heading of Aid to the Civil Power. This being so, the overall commander of FLAVIUS was the Gibraltar Police Commissioner Joseph Canepa and his orders were that the IRA active service unit was to be found and apprehended. To be quite precise, his orders were that the terrorists should be arrested and their arms and bombs made safe. This point is important both in view of what happened on the Rock and because the Spanish police along the Costa del Sol had managed to lose track of Farrell, McCann and Savage.

This was a setback but the pattern of the probable attack had already been worked out. The IRA would use two cars. One car, probably driven by Farrell, would enter the Rock and park on the route to the palace used by the band and troops. This car would be completely clean of explosives and its role was simply to occupy a space on the route to ensure that when the bomb car arrived it would have somewhere to park. The most likely spot was in the plaza where the troops and band assembled for the guard changing so close watch was kept there while the Spanish police scoured the Costa del Sol searching for the IRA terrorists and the bomb car. In spite of this the bomb car was not located and the IRA were able to park a white Renault 5 in the plaza on Gibraltar.

The scene now shifts to the afternoon of Sunday 5 March, 1988. Security was now at its height for on the following Tuesday morning the guard would be changed. The SAS troopers in plain clothes and armed with Browning 9 mm automatic pistols were working eight-hour shifts in teams of four and at about 2 p.m. the police reported that Savage had been spotted at a car in the plaza and 'fiddling with something inside the car'. The reasonable assumption was that he was priming an explosive charge for detonation by radio signal. At the same time another message reached the FLAVIUS operation HQ that Farrell and McCann had been spotted crossing the border and were walking up into the town.

In the next half hour there was a great deal of activity. An SAS explosive expert took a careful look at the car and reported that although nothing was certain, it probably contained a bomb. This was enough for the local police chief, Joseph Canepa, who duly signed the order passing the operation over into the hands of the SAS. This order was signed and timed at 1540 hours and the SAS then moved in on the IRA terrorists who were located walking back towards the border control post. By the airport Savage left the other two to walk on and started to walk back towards the town. By now four armed SAS troopers were within yards of the terrorists; two of them, identified as Soldiers A and B, continued with McCann and Farrell while two more, Soldiers C and D, shadowed Sean Savage. A few minutes later the shooting started.

The shooting seems to have been triggered accidentally by a police siren, coming from a vehicle which was attempting to get to where the SAS men were going to arrest the IRA. Traffic was heavy and the police switched on the siren in an attempt to clear a way. This sound close on their heels clearly alarmed the three, and McCann, looking round suddenly, made 'eye contact' with Soldier A about 30 feet behind him. It appears that both men came to a similar conclusion: McCann realised that the police or the security forces were on to them and Soldier A realised that he had been spotted. What happens then is more obscure.

According to SAS evidence given at the inquest McCann put his hand inside his jacket, perhaps to grab a pistol or trigger the firing device for the car bomb in the plaza. Taking no chances on either outcome, Soldier A drew his pistol and fired one round into McCann's back. Then – according to the evidence given at the inquest – seeing Farrell reach for her handbag, Soldier A fired one round into her as well. He then switched aim and put another bullet into McCann. Soldier B had meanwhile drawn his pistol and he fired a bullet into Maraid Farrell and another into McCann.

This burst of shooting was heard by the last IRA terrorist, Sean Savage who, again according to the evidence at the inquest, was seen to put his hand into his pocket. His shadowers, Soldiers C and D opened fire and shot him dead. At 1606 hours the SAS handed control of the incident back to the police chief, Joseph Canepa, and as far as the SAS were concerned the matter was finished. It was not to work out like that.

The British press were delighted with the Gibraltar affair. The public at large believed that a terrible tragedy had been averted and three terrorists, intent on a cowardly mass murder, had only got what was coming to them. Few tears were shed on the mainland for Farrell, McCann and Savage but then disquiet arose. This began on the following Monday afternoon when the Foreign Secretary got up in the House of Commons and in the course of a statement on the Gibraltar affair revealed that none of the terrorists were armed or had a triggering device and the car in the plaza did not contain a bomb.

This statement clashed with one issued just after the shootings – at 1645 hours on Sunday afternoon, which stated that, 'A suspected bomb has been found in Gibraltar and three suspects have been shot by civilian police.' This statement was issued within an hour of the shooting and a certain confusion about the details is understandable. At 2100 hours a further statement admitted that security forces had been involved in the shooting and had 'dealt with a suspect bomb'.

On the morning of Monday 7 March the Armed Forces Minister in London said on a radio programme that a large bomb had been found in Gibraltar and defused. This statement was incorrect. The bomb car – full of Semtex – was only located on the following day, Tuesday 8 March, 1988, in a car-park at Marbella on the Costa del Sol. The effect of these statement was unfortunate.

The Press, which had at first hailed the Gibraltar shootings with delight, now changed their tone completely and the SAS and the Government came in for a great deal of criticism, the first for the use of excessive force and the second for attempting a cover-up. It is only fair to add that a large proportion of the British public were also very unhappy about both the shooting and the cover-up confusion, and a TV programme, *Death on the Rock*, broadcast on 28 April which went into the affair in great detail only served to increase public disquiet.

To come to some reasonable conclusion is difficult. The fact that there was no bomb in the car in Gibraltar is not relevant; clearly the IRA were still at Phase One of their plan and the bomb car did exist, full of explosives, ready to be moved into place at some future time. There can be no reasonable doubt that the IRA fully intended a car bomb outrage in Gibraltar and their activists clearly had to be stopped. The question is, did they have to be killed?

Most people – and most soldiers – would feel that these three IRA terrorists were indiscriminate killers. Their relatives and supporters therefore had no grounds for complaint if McCann, Farrell and Savage were on the receiving end of some of their own tactics and no sympathy need be wasted there; had the terrorists succeeded in killing scores of people with their bomb then those who whined about the shooting would have rejoiced.

The main snag with that argument is that the British Government and its operatives are supposed to maintain the moral high ground and not operate a 'shoot to kill' policy. There is indeed no firm evidence that a shoot to kill 'policy' was ever sanctioned by the British Government and that accusation can be dismissed. That leaves only the matter of the actual shootings.

The official version, the one accepted by the Gibraltar inquest in September 1988 is given above and as a result of that inquest the coroner brought in a verdict of 'lawful killing'. This might have put an end to the speculation about what actually happened but the affair will not go away and attempts by sections of the Press and the Government to blacken the reputation of some of the witnesses only helped to keep speculation alive. The Government attempted to stop the showing of 'Death on the Rock' and sections of the Press went out of their way to blacken the character of one witness, Mrs Carmen Proetta, who lived in a flat overlooking the site of the shooting and according to her evidence, saw the whole thing.

According to Mrs Proetta, her attention was attracted to events across the road by two people putting their hands in the air. 'These people were turning their heads to see what was happening and when they saw these men with guns in their hands they put their hands up. It looked as if the man was protecting the girl because he stood in front of her but there was no chance.' According to her evidence the SAS 'jumped in with their guns in their hands and just went and shot these people. That's all.' Another witness claimed that Farrell and McCann were shot again while lying on the ground.

This evidence contradicts that given by the SAS troopers who claim that all three terrorists either put their hands to their pockets or in Farrell's case, into her handbag. Thinking they were reaching for weapons or the bomb trigger, the soldiers fired. The snag is that since the three did not have weapons or a bomb trigger, they had nothing to reach for.

A more natural reaction would be to raise their hands in the air which, according to Mrs Proetta, is exactly what they did do. It must be conceded that the sight of hands being put in the air is more likely to attract attention from a lady across the street than a hand reaching for a handbag or a pocket. It is worth mentioning that the British newspapers that attempted to dismiss Mrs Proetta's evidence by making attacks on her private reputation were later obliged to apologise and pay heavy sums in damages. Coming on top of the shooting of the Iranian terrorists after the ending of the Embassy siege, this incident left many people more than a little unhappy about the use of the SAS in a counter-terrorist role.

These two incidents bring into question why the British army – and specifically the SAS Regiment CRW team – is called in to handle incidents concerning small groups of terrorists. The streets of Gibraltar are not like the Radfan or the Malayan jungle where ambush is an acceptable tactic. While most democratic states now take steps to counter terrorist activity in the streets of their towns or at their airports the role of eliminating such groups is usually entrusted to specially trained police units. Only the British and the Dutch have elected to employ the military.

Every American police force contains a SWAT (Special Weapons and Tactics) team for use in the cases of hostage taking or sieges. The German police and the French gendarmerie have successfully wiped out terrorist gangs, the French most recently at Marseilles airport during Christmas 1994. During the same Christmas period armed response units of the British police shot and killed two people carrying firearms in the streets. Exactly why the SAS Regiment should be deployed when a gunman has a foreign accent or the title of terrorist is rather hard to determine and the SAS themselves may care to ponder exactly where this role is leading them.

16

SPORT AND SIDELINES

The official roles of the SAS – surveillance, small-scale operations, counter-terrorist warfare – have been restated at regular intervals throughout this book. Those are the roles for which the regiment is organised and for which it trains relentlessly at Hereford, in the surrounding hills and in other areas of the world. However, even in the SAS all work and no play makes Jack a dull soldier. The SAS men have therefore taken care to play games from time to time, usually those of the hard and dangerous variety.

Members of the regiment take part in the annual gruelling Devizes-to-Westminster 124 mile canoe race and any other difficult sporting challenge will usually attract a discreet entry or two from an address somewhere on the Welsh Marches. Freefall parachuting, rock-climbing and all-out mountaineering are other activities and the regiment has taken part in several ascents of Everest and other Himalayan peaks. Two SAS men, 'Brummie' Stokes and his companion 'Bronco' Lane took part in the 1970 Everest expedition and were lucky to escape with their lives after being forced to bivouac in the open on the way down from the summit. This has not stopped the pair returning to the mountains on many other occasions.

Rowing the Atlantic is not everyone's idea of a good time but John Ridgeway, who served in the SAS, and his sergeant Chay Blythe made the first successful crossing in a rowing boat and both have since gone on to circumnavigate the globe and take part in a wide range of fairly hazardous exploits. Another SAS man, Andy McLean, made the smallest small boat crossing of the Atlantic in 1982 in a craft just over nine feet long. As long as such challenges exist the SAS will find men eager to attempt them.

The regiment's reputation for well-honed survival skills has also attracted those civilians who are heading for the back of beyond on some hare-brained expedition and feel that a few tips from the men in the know will increase their chances of coming back in one piece.

Apart from these innocent activities and diversions SAS men have turned up in dangerous locations long after their period of service, either with the army or the regiment, was over. Many servicemen, and not only SAS men, find it difficult to settle down again when they return to civilian life and drift into other armies or such units as the Foreign Legion (which now operates not unlike the SAS) or into the service of other nations as 'contract officers'. Others find short-term but well-paid work as NCO instructors.

During the 1960s and 70s when the Europeans were leaving their various colonies in Africa there was a rash of local wars where white mercenaries took a leading role, most noticeably in the Belgian Congo and Katanga. A number of British ex-soldiers are serving with the armies fighting in the former Yugoslavia and inevitably some of them claim to have served with the SAS.

In any modern war, especially those fought in Africa, many of the mercenaries involved have claimed to have served in prestigious units like the SAS, a claim that may be taken with a very large pinch of salt. Though some SAS men probably have found employment in mercenary units – Colonel John Peters, who soldiered with Mile Hoare's 5 Commando in the Congo wars of the 1960s had served with the SAS in Malaya – most of those claiming an SAS background have never served in the regiment . . . which is not to say that some SAS men have not been willing to lend a friend a helping hand from time to time.

Johnny Cooper was 'one of the originals', a man who

joined the L Detachment of the SAS in the Kabrit days under David Stirling and rose to become Major J. Cooper, MBE DCM and a formidable fighting soldier. Johnny Cooper served throughout the war in the SAS and having tried civilian life for a brief while, rejoined and went to Malaya to serve in the Malayan Scouts where he was badly injured in a parachuting accident, breaking one arm in two places.

By 1960 John Cooper had finished his time with the SAS. He then went to the Oman to serve with the Northern Frontier Regiment, a contract that began with a few months in Aden learning Arabic, which Cooper picked up quite quickly. He then went on to serve with the Frontier Regiment, sparring with the Oman Liberation Army, an anti-Government group funded by Saudi Arabia. He was therefore well qualified by 1963 when David Stirling was looking for someone to organise some resistance in the Yemen to counteract the growing influence of Egypt and Arab nationalism.

Stirling's group had the backing of the British Foreign Office though on a strictly unofficial basis. Stirling's office in London in turn contacted Cooper, who requested a month's leave from his commanding officer, and met Stirling in Bahrain, where he was told that he was to lead a small Anglo-French force into the Yemen and find out what was going on. In fact Stirling intended to offer practical military help to the Royalist, pro-Western Yemeni forces but the official task was simply to observe and report on the extent of Egyptian involvement.

The Yemen was then engaged in a brisk little civil war between Royalist troops loyal to the present, vaguely pro-Western rulers, and the Egyptian inspired rebels who leaned towards a republic and were up to all kinds of tricks to eject the ruling family. One of the other things the Egyptians were certainly up to was encouraging the Yemenis to expel the British from Aden and the South Arabian protectorate. The British contingent for Cooper's eight-man team was provided – again on an unofficial basis – by the 22nd SAS Regiment.

There is something almost Victorian about this entire affair. This was a modern-day touch of the 'Great Game' played out on a new pitch and against a new enemy, though this was in the height of the cold war and anyone digging deeply into any anti-Western activity would eventually unearth a Russian.

Stirling was flitting about between Saudi Arabia and Aden and at the end of June 1963 Cooper's eight-man team crossed the frontier and made their way towards Sa'na, the capital of north Yemen, taking with them a large quantity of arms and ammunition loaded on 150 camels with which to earn the approval of the Royalist leader in Yemen, the Iman el Hassan. This trek took three weeks and was not without risk since the country had been extensively mined and control of the air was in the hands of the Egyptian air force.

Cooper and his troops began their campaign in support of the Royalist forces by laying on a major ambush, luring a large party of Egyptian troops onto a killing ground and shooting them up. The Egyptians duly located the Royalists, who were well dug in or in stone-walled 'sangars' and moved against them with a parachute battalion supported by tanks. The result was a massacre of the Egyptian infantry who were caught in a crossfire between the Royalists and Cooper's party and their own tanks. The Royalists killed a great many Egyptians and captured a large quantity of arms and ammunition after the Egyptians drew off.

Cooper remained in the Yemen for some time, overstaying his leave from the Frontier Regiment – as did the two SAS men in his force who were not particularly anxious to leave the field and get back to Hereford. It was very obvious that the rebellion in north Yemen was not only supported by Egypt but actually run by their troops.

Cooper and his team then made their way to south Yemen and back to London. After debriefing there Cooper returned to Aden only to have his aircraft diverted into Cairo by the Egyptian air traffic control. When the aircraft landed, Egyptian officials came on board and said that, since the aircraft was 'overweight', Mr Cooper would have to get off. Clearly Cooper's involvement in the Yemen – and his presence on the aircraft – were known to the Egyptian military. Cooper duly disembarked and was thoroughly searched by Egyptian intelligence officers but they failed to find anything to detain him for and he was released and flew on to Aden.

From Aden Cooper went back to north Yemen again by camel, this time taking with him a large quantity of gold and a powerful radio. This tour of unofficial duty got off to a very bad start when the Egyptians located the radio base and attacked it with chemical weapons – nerve gas – and blinding one of the French radio operators.

Cooper remained in the Yemeni mountains for the next nine months, building up full details of the Egyptian army strengths, sending useful items of captured Soviet equipment back to England, and organising air drops of supplies, weapons and ammunition to the Royalist forces. He also continued the long-standing SAS hearts and minds role, offering medical aid to the hill people, contracting tuberculosis himself in the process. He was eventually joined by more British volunteers, including a soldier from the 21 SAS Regiment.

By this time stories of British involvement in Yemeni affairs were appearing in the British newspapers, running stories fed to them by Egyptian intelligence. When Cooper returned to Britain he was chased about by reporters anxious for information and records that he was very glad to 'return to the quiet life in the Yemeni mountains'.

Life in the Yemeni mountains hardly seems dull but visitors kept dropping in, including the explorer Wilfred Thesinger who had been with the SAS L Detachment in 1942, undeterred by the fact that the Egyptian air force were still roving at will over the Yemeni skies, attacking anything that moved with heavy bombs, rockets and machine-guns. Cooper's 'one month leave' from the Frontier Regiment lasted for three years, until 1966 when he returned to the regiment only to discover that he had TB and had to spend the next two years getting over it.

Cooper's small war in the Yemen was not exactly typical

of SAS operations but there are plenty of other examples of SAS troopers being detached alone or in small groups to different parts of the world. The regiment has taken an active part in guarding British Embassies in an increasingly unstable world, or in training local guards in security, both for the Embassy building and the Embassy staff. From this it was a natural step to providing guards for foreign rulers, or instructing the guards of friendly rulers in the finer points of security.

This last role began the regiment's involvement in plain clothes operations, a role that began in Aden in 1966. The regiment had been involved in actions in the Radfan, though the bulk of the fighting there was handled by 45 Commando, Royal Marines and the Parachute Regiment. Both these units also became involved in the fighting in and around Aden and Little Aden as the British began to withdraw. Sensing that the British were on their way out, the Arabs (in what time they had to spare from fighting each other) began to snipe and shoot at British troops on foot or Land Rover patrol, inflicting a number of casualties.

In an attempt to discourage this activity SAS Major Peter de la Billiere, who had been involved in the Oman fighting and was to later command all the British forces present in Saudi Arabia and Iraq during the Gulf War, set up a training school in Aden, where his men honed up on their pistol-shooting skills and were then sent out in plain clothes to roam the streets of Aden in the hope that the terrorist gunmen would strike at them and be shot down.

The SAS were not operating a shoot-to-kill policy because the initiative for the attacks rested with the terrorists, but the underlying strategy was to fight fire with fire, and meet terrorism with counter-terrorism. It cannot be said that this policy was successful. The technique, which became known as 'Keeni-meeni work' did not draw many gunmen into action and almost inevitably led to an accidental encounter between a plain clothed patrol of SAS and a uniformed patrol of the Royal Anglian Regiment. Fortunately, no one was injured in the exchange of fire.

Counter-terrorism began to occupy more and more of the SAS Regiment's attention throughout the 1970s when terrorists of various kinds, ranging from urban guerrillas of the Baader–Meinhof and Red Brigade variety to the anti-Zionist Arab variety, were active in many parts of the world, usually directing their activities against innocent civilians, unsuspecting military bases and civil aircraft.

In this type of warfare the initiative always lies with the terrorist and the only answer, apart from sound intelligence information, is a swift response. A good example of the latter came in May 1972 when a bomb was reported on board the luxury liner *Queen Elizabeth II*, then in mid-Atlantic. Within an hour of the threat being known a small bomb disposal team from the Royal Marines, the Royal Engineers and the SAS was on its way.

These men parachuted into the Atlantic over the liner, were picked up by small boats and carried out a thorough check of the ship which continued to steam at full speed for the nearest port. No bomb was found, but the lessons learned proved useful in later terrorist alarms, when the SAS team on standby at Hereford was *en route* to the incident within minutes.

This chapter has illustrated a wide number of SAS activities, from taking part in mountaineering expeditions to fighting terrorists in the back streets and souks of Arabia, to clandestine operations where the British had no wish to make a formal intervention. The SAS had a useful part to play in all these activities but the thrust of the unit was increasingly towards the counter-terrorist role, a task that carries great dangers and considerable political risks.

17

THE SAS IN 'DESERT STORM'

The Gulf War of 1990–1 will probably go down in the annals of military history as a very curious little war indeed. It began when the dictator of Iraq, Saddam Hussein invaded the tiny sheikdom of Kuwait on 2 August 1990, and a large combination of other nations led by the United States and operating under the banner of the United Nations set out to expel him.

The official reason for this international response was to deter other dictators from similar acts and to introduce a 'New World Order' following the collapse of the USSR and the familiar Cold War verities. A more honest reason was desire to protect and secure the vast oil reserves of Kuwait and Saudi Arabia.

In the months that followed Saddam Hussein qualified for the title of 'Dictator of the Decade' award as he prevaricated and temporised, running rings round the leaders of the Western Alliance while a build-up of coalition forces went on in Saudi Arabi and politicians sought a peaceful solution.

The actual fighting, Saddam Hussein's much vaunted and long promised 'Mother of Battles', the Allied 'Desert Storm' offensive, did not begin until Thursday 17 January 1991. The first phase was the air war, with massive aircraft and cruise missile attacks on Baghdad and military targets in Iraq. Air attacks continued for some weeks, wrecking Iraq and pounding her army to pieces while the Allied navies roamed up the coast, sinking Iraqi shipping, clearing mines and launching cruise missiles. Only when the Iraqi forces had been severely pummelled did the ground war begin.

The ground troops advanced at 0400 hours on Sunday 24 February 1991, with two massive armoured thrusts across the Iraqi border and two days later, on 26 February 1991, the Gulf War was over. The ending of the war was inconclusive for Saddam Hussein still rules in Iraq and the threat he is said to have posed still exists today.

The 'Desert Storm' operation threw up some strange statistics. The largest source of American casualties came not in combat but from traffic accidents during the months of the build-up. The largest number of British casualties were caused by the Americans in 'friendly fire' accidents. This very brief war, largely fought in the air or with missiles, produced no less than five bestselling books. One of them, *Bravo Two Zero* has been on the bestseller lists for two years and the author, Andy McNab DCM MM should now be rich enough to buy his own army.

The war was also remarkable for the growing influence of the television media which operated seemingly at will on both sides of the lines. Very senior generals apparently found it necessary to return from their duties in the desert to answer questions raised by an ever larger press corps.

A great many pundits were dug out of retirement to opine on the outcome of the struggle and forecast woe to the Allies at the hands of the Iraqi 'elite' Republican Guard. When push came to shove the 'elite' Republican Guard – the word 'elite' was never omitted by Western correspondents – fled from the battle as fast as their transport would take them.

Since much of the official documentation covering 'Desert Storm' is still embargoed, this account rests on TV recordings made at the time and extensive newspaper files. The SAS role remains surrounded in a certain amount of mystery regarding the actual details of their activities other than those vividly described by Andy McNab in *Bravo Two Zero*. What can be said is that the SAS saw more action than other ground forces involved and were out in the desert, moving behind the Iraqi lines, even before the air war began.

Special forces other than the SAS did not get much of a showing during Desert Storm. This caused a certain amount of angst at Aldershot and Plymouth where the Parachute Regiment battalions and the 3rd Commando Brigade, Royal Marines were anxious to be committed. Indeed, one very senior Royal Marine officer remarked to this author that it was 'very bad manners to give a war and not invite Her Majesty's Royal Marines'.

In fact the first ground action of the war was a small raid by Royal Marines of the Special Boat Service on 23 January when the SBS went in and blew up a large section of the communication link between Saddam's bunker HQ in Baghdad and the Iraqi front-line positions. This group was flown in by night in Chinook helicopters to a position in the desert 40 miles from Baghdad. Having landed they dug up the cables, removed a large section and flew out again without loss. Otherwise the SBS were also tasked with re-entering Kuwait as soon as the main battle was over, to reoccupy the British Embassy.

It was clear from the outset that the war against Iraq would be largely an air war or a war of heavy armoured units, where Western weapons and advanced military technology could be brought to bear against Iraq's large infantry forces.

The SAS however, were born in the desert 50 years before Desert Storm. In many ways the regiment was returning to its birthplace, albeit a few thousand miles further east. The SAS were even equipped for this operation in a similar way. Long-wheel-based Land Rovers replaced the traditional Willis Jeep and the GPMG (general purpose machine-gun) was mounted in place of the Bren or the Vickers 'K' but otherwise not a lot had changed since the desert campaigns of half a century before. The regiment had several squadrons in the field by early December and were presented with three possible tasks.

The first was to rescue Western hostages held in Kuwait, the second was to interdict the MSRs (Major

Supply Routes) and the last, and in the end by far the most important, was to find and destroy the Iraqi Scud missiles. Each of these tasks can now be described in detail.

When the Iraqi forces rolled in, Kuwait contained a very large number of British and Western expatriates plus, by some accident, the passengers and crew of a British Airways jet which landed at Kuwait when the invasion was actually in progress and was unable to get away.

Some of these expatriates had a very bad time indeed and in an attempt to secure the more vital installations against coalition air attacks Saddam sent a number of his expatriate prisoners to each installation as hostages – human shields – letting it be known that if these places were attacked or bombed, the Western hostages, men, women and children, would be the first to die.

In the end, most of these hostages were in fact released as a stream of Western diplomats and politicians went to see Saddam, heard his story and were rewarded for their peacemaking efforts with a handful of hostages. Since these people had elected to work and live in a very unstable part of the world it is not likely that their presence on the ground would have delayed the outcome of the war but it would have been better if the majority could have been removed to a place of safety before the campaign began.

This was no easy task, as the American special forces had discovered some years before in 1982 when the Iranians invaded their Embassy in Teheran and took the staff hostage. An attempt to rescue the hostages by helicopter ended in a costly disaster and the chances of something more effective being put into place this time were not too good, not least because of the numbers involved and the difficulty of finding their exact whereabouts. In the end, convinced perhaps that holding hostages did his cause no good, Saddam Hussein released all his Western prisoners on 8 December and most of them were home before the action started.

The British commander in Saudi Arabia, General Sir

Peter de la Billiere, a former SAS officer, had decreed that the SAS would only be deployed if there was a task suitable to their talents that could not be performed equally well by some other means, and that the SAS troopers, if committed behind the Iraqi lines, could be safely extracted when their task was done. By mid-January General de la Billiere had located two such tasks and the SAS duly went out into the Iraqi-held desert charged with attacking Iraqi road transport and communication links and creating diversions. This task was to begin as soon as the air war commenced.

The air war duly commenced on 17 January and the SAS went out into the desert three days later on 20 January. Six days later the SAS met a major setback when one of their patrols was located and attacked by the Iraqis and eight men went missing. Meanwhile however, the SAS had become involved in a very critical affair: the war of the Scuds.

The Scud is a medium-range tactical missile, just under 40 feet long, carrying either an explosive or a nuclear warhead – the ones deployed by Iraq were of the conventional kind. They could be fired from fixed sites or mobile transporters and if they were deployed against targets in Israel they had a range of between 100 and 175 miles. This was a useful piece of information for it meant that to range freely against targets in Israel the Scuds must be launched as close to Israel as possible and could not be hidden all over Iraq.

One of the main problems facing the West was keeping the other Arab nations out of the war. Arab and Muslim communities all over the world – including those in the UK – were largely behind Saddam, seeing him as their leader in the fight against the decadence and ungodliness of the West, whatever their leaders, rulers and politicians might feel. Even these might go over to Saddam's side if he could present his war as part of the struggle against the arch-enemy, Israel.

For their part the Israelis made it plain that if the West failed to sort Saddam out they would do so themselves, in

173

very short order and without more of this pussyfooting about. This was a heady, volatile brew for if Israel did enter the war most of the Arab nations would be obliged to side with Saddam. Saddam therefore had every reason to provoke Israel and he had the means to do it, for his Scud missiles had the range to reach major civilian targets in Israel.

On the night of 17 January, the night the air war began, he launched eight Scud missiles against Israel; two hit Haifa and four landed in Tel Aviv, causing more than 100 civilian casualties. Within minutes war planes of the formidable Israeli air force were in the air and heading for Baghdad.

Heavy pressure, mostly from Washington, made the Israelis hold their fire for the moment but it was clear that unless the Scuds could be found and destroyed, the Israelis would come into the war. The fixed Scud missile sites could be found and attacked by the wide-ranging Allied air forces; the far more difficult task of locating and destroying the mobile missile launchers was given to the SAS.

The SAS teams were deployed in a vast area which became known as the 'Scud Box'. Roaming around in this area in desert vehicles, these teams began to locate the missile launchers and call down air strikes. The only problem was that calling in a strike and passing on the necessary co-ordinates took time, and with the mobile missile launchers able to move within minutes these air strikes were not as successful as they might have been.

After a few Scuds had got away, the SAS took to engaging the missile launchers with heavy machine-guns or Milan anti-tank missiles; they also attacked communication and radar installations controlling Scud missile operations. This proved highly effective but merely confirmed what the Iraqis were beginning to suspect anyway; that the SAS were on the ground behind their lines and would have to be rooted out.

The SAS teams were having their own problems. The desert is not always the sun-kissed hot environment of

Beau Geste stories and it was winter in Iraq. The teams were hit by blizzards and very low temperatures mingled in with sandstorms and fog. This itself was very testing and as the days went by the SAS teams came under increasing pressure from roving Iraqi patrols.

The SAS were easier to find than they were in the Western Desert during World War II because to find their targets they were obliged to stay close to the Iraqi main supply routes – the metalled roads and firm tracks which were capable of supporting the passage of the heavy, long Scud missile transporters. Striking at the MSRs proved risky but very effective and there were no successful missile strikes against Israel after 24 January.

Precise details of the raids and attacks made against the Scuds may not be known for a long time, if ever, but the main stories coming out of the SAS involvement in Desert Storm come from those SAS men who were cut off during the course of these attacks and either made their way to friendly territory or were picked up by Saddam's troops and put through a harrowing ordeal.

The full story of what happened to Andy McNab and two men of his team has been told by the man himself in the excellent *Bravo Two Zero*. Briefly, his team were put through brutal interrogations before being released into the hands of the Red Cross on 5 March. Another SAS soldier walked nearly 200 miles to safety across the enemy-thronged desert and into Syria before being picked up and taken to the British Embassy in Damascus.

The bodies of four SAS men killed in these operations against the Scuds or the MSRs were eventually returned by the Iraqis and a number of awards, some of them posthumous, were awarded to the regiment for their actions in the Gulf War.

With the collapse of Communism and the break up of Yugoslavia and the Soviet Union, the old Cold War 'enemies' have either disappeared or been eclipsed. That is not to say that the world has got any safer; indeed, many world leaders and politicians feel that the world has become increasingly unstable, and that new threats will arise, probably in the Middle East, or as a result of instability in the Balkans. The drift of people from the Third World into Europe and North America may also present a problem, and the continuing anarchy in Africa is unlikely to moderate in the coming decades.

In the middle of all this uncertainty, the Western world is seeking a 'Peace Dividend', by reducing its armed forces and the development of new weapons. How far this can go in these uncertain times is a matter of judgement, but it seems likely that there will always be a need for small, hard-hitting units who can adapt to changing circumstances and provide the political leaders with a forceful answer when all else fails. The SAS Regiment has been providing such a service for more than 50 years, and is willing to go on doing it, for many years to come.

BIBLIOGRAPHY

The Battle for the Falklands, Max Hastings and Simon Jenkins (Michael Joseph, 1983)

Bravo Two Zero, Andy McNab DCM MM (Corgi Books, 1994)

Eastern Approaches, Fitzroy Maclean (Cape, 1949)

Fighting General: the Public and Private Campaigns of General Sir Walter Walker, Tom Pocock (Collins, 1973)

Four Five, David Young (Leo Cooper, 1972)

Last Post: Aden 1964–67, J. Paget (Faber, 1969)

One of the Originals, Johnny Cooper (Pan Books, 1991)

Operation Tombola, Roy Farran (Collins, 1960)

The Phantom Major, Virginia Cowles (Collins, 1958)

The SAS, Philip Warner (Sphere, 1983)

SAS: The Jungle Frontier, Peter Dickens (Fontana Books, 1984)

SAS: Operation Oman, Col Tony Jeapes (William Kimber, 1980)

The SAS: Savage Wars of Peace, Anthony Kemp (John Murray, 1994)

The SBA, Philip Warner (Sphere, 1983)

SBS in World War Two, G. B. Courtney (Robert Hale, 1983)

Storm Command, General Sir Peter de la Billiere (Harper Collins, 1993)

This is the SAS, Tony Geraghty (Arms and Armour Press, 1982)

The Weapons of Terror, C. Dogson and R. Payne (Macmillan, 1979)

Who Dares Wins, Tony Geraghty (Arms and Armour Press, 1980)

Winged Dagger, Roy Farran (Elmfield Press, 1973)